Patrick Madrid

Any Friend of God's
Is A Friend of Mine

"God has so adjusted the body . . . that there
may be no discord in the body, but that the
members may have the same care for one another.
If one member suffers, all suffer together.
If one member is honored, all rejoice together."
(1 Cor. 12:24-26)

❖

¡Viva Nuestra Señora de Guadalupe!

With love and thanks to Nancy
and our own little "cloud of witnesses":
Jonathon, Bridget, Timothy, Hillary, Maximilian,
Madeline, Judith, Augustine, and Baby Number Nine.

Patrick Madrid

Any Friend of God's Is A Friend of Mine

A Biblical and Historical Explanation of the
Catholic Doctrine of the Communion of Saints

Basilica Press ❖ San Diego

— Contents —

Introduction — 7

Chapter One — 11
What is the Communion of Saints?

Chapter Two — 17
Classical Protestant Objections

Chapter Three — 27
"Me and Jesus" Christianity Isn't Biblical

Chapter Four — 43
The "One Mediator" Argument and Other Objections

Chapter Five — 67
Praying for the Souls in Purgatory

Chapter Six — 77
The Testimony of the Early Church

Chapter Seven — 89
The Veneration of Relics

Chapter Eight — 95
Statues and Images

Chapter Nine — 101
Does Honoring Mary and the Saints Offend God?

Appendix — 117
Council of Trent: "Decree Concerning the Invocation,
Veneration, and Relics of Saints and Sacred Images"

Introduction

DOES OUR HONORING and invoking the intercession of Mary and the saints make God jealous? No.
As the Bible says, they are His friends and, therefore,
they should be our friends.

You and I cannot bestow any honor upon them
higher than the ones the Lord has already bestowed
on them.[1] We ask for their intercessory prayer just
as we ask other Christians here on earth, and their
intercession on our behalf is "good and pleasing to
God our Savior."[2]

We reverence their relics and sacred images because they remind us of these real men and women
who loved God so greatly. Mary and the saints are
our models in faith. They teach us what it means to
love and follow and obey Christ.[3] Their bodies were
temples of the Holy Spirit[4] and they reign now in
royal glory with the Blessed Trinity as priests and

---

[1] Luke 1:46-49; 1 Cor. 2:9.
[2] 1 Tim. 2:1-4.
[3] 1 Cor. 11:1; Phil. 3:17, 4:9; 1 Thess. 1:6.
[4] 1 Cor. 3:16-17; 6:19-20.

kings forever.[5]

The difference between the Catholic and Protestant views on this subject can best be illustrated with this analogy. Imagine you are visiting a king. As you are being shown into His royal throne room you notice immediately the beautiful music lilting through the air. As you step into the chamber you are dazzled by the beauty of the place: Gorgeous tapestries hang from the walls, stunning works of art adorn the room, sumptuous carpet covers the floor. You see men and women dressed in splendid apparel, their faces shining with happiness, their countenances beautiful to behold.

As you progress further into the room, towards the King, you realize that the grandeur in the room grows accordingly. Finally, you reach the foot of the throne, and you gaze upon the King Himself. He is magnificent, far more glorious than anything or anyone in the room. You're overwhelmed by the regal beauty of His clothing, His crown, His scepter, His throne. But the King Himself is the center, the focal point of all the glory that surrounds Him. You can see that this king lavishes His wealth and love for beauty on everything that surrounds Him.

Now, imagine you're entering the throne room of a different king.

The first thing you notice is the absence of sound. There is no music. There are no exquisite tapestries to catch your eye, no works of art, no jewel-studded carpet. There are no people here. In fact, there is literally nothing in the room that could

---

[5] Rev. 1:6, 5-10.

conceivably distract your attention from the King, Who sits in magnificent glory on His throne, at the far end of the room. Why is this room bare of all ornaments and empty of courtiers? Because this King is jealous of His glory. He doesn't want you to become distracted by anything else — He wants you to see only Himself.

Which king is more glorious? Obviously the first. These two kings represent the two very different ways that Catholics and Protestants understand God's attitude toward His creatures.

The example of the second King is characteristic of the Protestant conception. This King will allow nothing else to attract your attention, even if just for a moment. True, He is a glorious King, but doesn't His throne room seem drab and empty?

The first King represents how Catholics see God and His attitude toward His friends. Because He Himself is glorious, He lavishes glory on everyone and everything that surrounds Him. He is not worried that you will focus for a moment on the beauty of a tapestry or the splendid garb of one of His courtier friends. That you do marvel at these glorious peripheral items in itself gives greater honor and glory to Him. The glory that suffuses everything around this King is evidence of His own glory. It highlights this fact and pulls our attention always and inexorably to the focus of all: Him.

The Catholic model of the communion of saints is the biblical model. Because we love God, we love His friends. And we know that because God loves us, His friends love us, too. — *PM*

One

What Is the Communion of Saints?

EVERY SUNDAY millions of Christians recite the Apostles Creed, professing their belief in the "communion of saints." Few realize the importance of this phrase, sandwiched as it is between other deep mysteries of the Catholic Faith.

Historically, Protestants have denounced the Catholic teaching on the communion of saints as "unbiblical." It's a bitter irony that the very doctrine of Christian unity has itself become a barrier to unity. The controversy revolves around the question, "Is it biblical to ask the saints in heaven to pray (intercede) for us?"

Catholics say yes. They recognize that since Christians are united with each other through Christ, and are commanded to love and pray for one another, Christians on earth can ask Christians in heaven for their prayers.

Protestants say no. They argue that praying to saints undermines Christ's unique mediatorship, pointing to 1 Timothy 2:5: "There is one God and one mediator between God and men, the man Christ Jesus." They think asking the saints to intercede for us is in direct conflict with this verse.

As with the various other Catholic doctrines Protestants oppose, there is a fundamental misunderstanding by Protestants about the Catholic teaching on this subject. They worry that by praying to Mary and the saints, Catholics are *worshipping* them; that giving honor to the saints is actually robbing honor from God; and that using crucifixes, icons, statues, and other holy images of Christ, Mary, and the saints, is just a Catholic form of idolatry. But these are misunderstandings — ones we Catholics have an obligation to clear up.

Since Evangelicals are Bible-oriented in their approach to doctrinal matters (we Catholics should take a cue from them and become more Bible-oriented ourselves), it's crucial that we know how to explain the basics of the communion of saints from the Bible. We must also show them the historical evidence for this doctrine from the writings and liturgical practices of the early Church.

That's why I wrote this book. It's designed to help Catholics understand the various arguments raised by Protestants against this Catholic teaching and know how to respond to them. I give special attention to the biblical and historical evidence for the communion of saints — particularly, why we invoke the intercession of Mary and the saints — as well as the subsidiary issues of the veneration of relics, and the pious use of sacred images, icons, and statues. (This book does not deal with Marian doctrines *per se*, eg. the Immaculate Conception, the Assumption, Our Lady's Perpetual Virginity, etc.)

It's my hope that this book will be a handy tool for the Catholic who wishes to explain and defend these fundamental truths of our Holy Faith.

The Catholic Teaching

There are a number of sources one could turn to for a detailed explanation of what we mean by the "communion of saints," but the best by far is the *Catechism of the Catholic Church* (CCC). Paragraphs 946-92 provide a basic outline of the doctrine, and one of the key phrases is this one:

> "The term 'communion of saints' therefore has two closely linked meanings: communion 'in holy things (*sancta*)' and 'among holy persons (*sancti*).'"[6]

Since the communion of saints is, at its essence, the doctrine of the nature of the Church, this definition points us toward a two-fold reality about the Church. First, as members of the Body of Christ, all Christians enjoy a communion in faith, fellowship, the sacraments, liturgies, and all the other spiritual goods poured out on the Church by Christ. Second, because they are members of the Body of Christ, all Christians enjoy a real (not figurative) communion,

---

[6] CCC 948.

a literal organic unity with Christ and *with each other*. This unity, as we shall see in coming chapters, extends across time and space and is not severed by death. It is the core of the doctrine of the communion of saints.

Vatican II outlined the essential theological elements of the Catholic teaching. It's well worth reading slowly and carefully:

> "By the hidden and kindly mystery of God's will, a supernatural solidarity reigns among men. A consequence of this is that the sin of one person harms other people just as one person's holiness helps others. In this way, Christian believers help each other reach their supernatural destiny . . .
>
> "This is the very ancient dogma called the communion of saints. It means that the life of each individual son of God is joined in Christ and through Christ by a wonderful link to the life of all his other Christian brethren. Together they form the supernatural unity of Christ's Mystical Body so that, as it were, a single mystical person is formed . . . The union of the living with their brethren who have fallen asleep in Christ is not broken; the Church has rather believed through the ages that it gains strength from the sharing of spiritual benefits. The great intimacy of the union of those in heaven with Christ gives extra steadiness in holiness to the whole Church and makes a manifold contribution to the extension of her building. Now that they are welcomed in their own country and are at home with the Lord, through Him, with Him, and in Him, they intercede unremittingly with the Father on our behalf."[7]

---

[7] *Sacrosanctum Concilium*, 4-5; cf. CCC 946-952.

From this explanation, we can see that the doctrine of the communion of saints permeates virtually
every aspect of Catholic teaching. In other words, an
authentic understanding of the nature of the Church,
its liturgy and sacraments, the Lord's plan of salvation, indeed the very redemptive mission of Christ
Himself, is dependent in various ways upon an ac-
curate understanding of what the Creed means
when it says, "I believe in the communion of
saints."[8]

As we'll see in coming chapters, this communion extends beyond mere temporal, earthly fellowship. It involves, as the *Catechism* says, a
communication of spiritual goods. This means it includes intercessory prayers and, in a secondary way,
the entire panoply of honoring and venerating God's
friends. We on earth venerate our brothers and sisters in heaven, the saints, precisely because the
Lord showers them with unimaginable honor and
glory. The communion of saints involves our participation in Christ's honoring of the Blessed Virgin
Mary and the saints.[9]

The communion of saints is a broad subject, but
not a particularly complex one: We who are united
with Christ through baptism are intimately united to
each other. All the benefits, joys, and obligations
that flow from this relationship form the various elements of the doctrine of the communion of saints.

The difficulty between Protestants and Catholics
arises here. Protestants will agree that there is a

---

[8] Cf. CCC 787, 946-962.
[9] Cf. Rom. 1:9-12, 15:30-32; Eph. 6:18-20.

unity, but they will not go along with the necessary implications the Catholic Church draws from that fact: a) This unity in Christ transcends time and space; b) It involves all Christians, in heaven, on earth, and in purgatory; c) It is a unity that, by its very nature, involves for all concerned an obligation of charity and mutual support.

We'll examine various aspects of the communion of saints, such as praying to them, honoring them, venerating their relics, and the use of icons and statues. As we go along, we'll also analyze the major Protestant arguments against these Catholic teachings and practices.

Two

Classical Protestant Objections

IT'S WORTH LOOKING at some representative examples of formal Protestant statements issued at the time of the Reformation to get a feel for why Protestants reject this Catholic teaching.

Contemporary American Evangelical theology has in many respects drifted away from its original, Reformation-era forms. This is due, at least in part, to the vast and pervasive influence of Anabaptist theology that has subtly shaped, and in some cases literally obliterated, the theological contours of "classical" denominations, such as Lutheranism and the Reformed churches.

The rough-and-ready and not terribly systematic theologies of today's "non-denominational," "full gospel," "independent," and "Bible-believing" denominations, have managed to give many American

Protestants the misimpression that their theology is identical with that of their Reformation forefathers. But this is not the case. Contemporary Evangelicalism has departed in many respects from its Reformation sources, and so has its reaction to certain Catholic teachings. Most Evangelicals today heartily believe in (even if they don't fully understand) Martin Luther's formulas of *sola fide* (justification by faith alone) and *sola scriptura* (by Scripture alone), but they differ with the Reformers on certain points. For example, Martin Luther and John Calvin both were staunch defenders of the Catholic doctrine of Mary's perpetual virginity.[10] Both dismissed the arguments raised to the contrary as ludicrous and, ironically, "unbiblical." Yet today, attacking Mary's perpetual virginity is *de rigueur* among Evangelicals.

But on the communion of saints, today's Protestants have not drifted much from the objections the Reformers gave. To get a clear picture of the arguments, let's examine several that were raised at the time of the Reformation.

The Anglicans, under the leadership of Thomas Cranmer, Archbishop of Canterbury, argued,

"The Romish doctrine concerning . . . [the] invocation of saints is a fond thing, vainly invented, and grounded upon no warranty of Scripture, but is,

---

[10] Luther's and Calvin's views on Mary's perpetual virginity and other Marian doctrines are summarized in Michael O'Carrol, *Dictionary of Marian Theology*, (Collegeville: Michael Glazier Press, 1988), 92-94.

rather, repugnant to the Word of God."[11]

In 1530, Protestant apologist Philip Melanchthon (1497-1560) summarized the Lutheran objection:

"It is also taught among us that saints should be kept in remembrance so that our faith may be strengthened when we see what grace they received and how they were sustained by faith. Moreover, their good works are to be an example for us, each of us in his own calling. So His Imperial Majesty may in salutary and godly fashion imitate the example of David in making war on the Turk, for both are incumbents of a royal office which demands the defense and protection of their subjects. However, *it cannot be proved from the Scriptures that we are to invoke the saints or seek help from them.* 'For there is one mediator between God and men, Christ Jesus' (1 Tim. 2:5), who is the only savior, the only high priest, advocate, and intercessor before God. He alone has promised to hear our prayers. Moreover, according to the Scriptures, the highest form of divine service is sincerely to seek and call upon this same Jesus Christ in every time of need." [12]

John Calvin (1509-1564), the founder of the Reformed wing of Protestantism, shows the same skittishness about the role of the saints that marks all the standard Protestant arguments on this subject. In this passage (lengthy, but worth quoting in its entirety, in order to get the full flavor of his argument),

---

[11] *39 Articles of Religion*, article 22.

[12] *The Augsburg Confession,* article 21 (translated from the German recension), *The Book of Concord*, Theodore G. Tappert, translator, editor (Philadelphia: Fortress Press, 1959), 46-47. Emphasis added.

note particularly Calvin's tragic misunderstanding of the Catholic position, and his "straw man"[13] fallacious argument regarding Christ being the One Mediator, spoken of in 1 Timothy 2:5:

"In regard to the saints who having died in the body live in Christ, if we attribute prayer to them, let us not imagine that they have any other way of supplicating God than through Christ who alone is the way, or that their prayers are accepted by God in any other name. *Wherefore, since the Scripture calls us away from all others to Christ alone, since our heavenly Father is pleased to gather together all things in him, it were the extreme of stupidity, not to say madness, to attempt to obtain access by means of others, so as to be drawn away from him without whom access cannot be obtained.* But who can deny that this was the practice for several ages, and is still the practice, wherever Popery prevails? To procure the favor of God, human merits are ever and anon obtruded [ie. always looked to], *and very frequently while Christ is passed by, God is supplicated in their name. I ask if this is not to transfer to them that office of sole intercession which we have above claimed for Christ?* Then what angel or devil ever announced one syllable to any human being concerning that fancied intercession of

---

[13] The straw man fallacy "is committed when the arguer distorts an opponent's position for the purpose of more easily attacking it, demolishes the distorted argument, and then proceeds to conclude that the opponent's real argument has been demolished. By so doing the arguer is said to have set up a straw man and knocked it down, only to conclude that the real man (opposing argument) has been knocked down as well." Patrick J. Hurley, *A Concise Introduction to Logic* (Belmont, CA: Wadsworth Publishing Co., 1994), 124.

theirs?

"There is not a word on the subject in Scripture. What ground then was there for the fiction? Certainly, while the human mind thus seeks help for itself in which it is not sanctioned by the word of God, it plainly manifests its distrust. But if we appeal to the consciences of all who take pleasure in the intercession of saints, we shall find that *their only reason for it is, that they are filled with anxiety, as if they supposed that Christ were insufficient or too rigorous.* By this anxiety they dishonor Christ, and rob him of his title of sole Mediator, a title which being given him by the Father as his special privilege, ought not to be transferred to any other. By so doing they obscure the glory of his nativity and make void his cross; in short, divest and defraud of due praise everything which he did or suffered, since all which he did and suffered goes to show that he is and ought to be deemed sole Mediator." [14]

Calvin flails away here at everything except the actual Catholic teaching. The Catholic Church does *not* teach that the saints have some "special way" to intercede for us outside of or separate from Christ's mediatorship. The Catholic Church has always emphasized that the intercession of Mary and the saints, like that of any Christian, is solely reliant upon and always subordinate to the unique role of Christ as the One Mediator (cf. 1 Tim. 2:5). For Calvin to make this assertion shows either an inexcusable ignorance of the Catholic doctrine he seeks to rebut, or ill will, or both.

---

[14] *Institutes of the Christian Religion*, 28:21.

Notice his claim that:

"If we appeal to the consciences of all who take pleasure in the intercession of saints, we shall find that their only reason for it is, that they are filled with anxiety, as if they supposed that Christ were insufficient or too rigorous."[15]

The main problem with this line of argumentation is obvious: Calvin is inconsistent. If asking for the intercession of the saints in heaven evidences an attitude that Christ's mediation is "insufficient or too rigorous," then asking any Christian here on earth for intercessory prayer is likewise an indictment of the sufficiency of Christ's mediation. Yet Calvin (like all Protestants), rightly allowed for and even extolled the practice of Christians on earth offering intercessory prayers for each other. Clearly, asking another Christian for intercessory prayer in no way indicates any lack of confidence in Christ. His "we don't see *that* in the Bible" argument for rejecting the Catholic view of the communion of saints, among other doctrines, is typical of the Protestant approach to Catholic teaching[16] and will be dealt with in the next chapter, where we'll examine the biblical evidence in support of this Catholic teaching.

Calvin continues his critique:

"At the same time, they [Catholics] reject the kindness of God in manifesting himself to them as a

---

[15] Ibid.

[16] A perfect example of this stunted *sola scriptura* reasoning is found in James G. MCarthy, *The Gospel According to Rome* (Eugene: Harvest House, 1995), 206-207.

Father, for he is not their Father if they do not recognize Christ as their brother. This they plainly refuse to do if they think not that he feels for them a brother's affection; affection than which none can be more gentle or tender. Wherefore Scripture offers him alone, sends us to him, and establishes us in him. 'He,' says Ambrose, 'is our mouth by which we speak to the Father; our eye by which we see the Father; our right hand by which we offer ourselves to the Father. Save by his intercession neither we nor any saints have any intercourse with God.' If they object that the public prayers which are offered up in churches conclude with the words, 'through Jesus Christ our Lord,' it is a frivolous evasion; because no less insult is offered to the intercession of Christ by confounding it with the prayers and merits of the dead, than by omitting it altogether, and making mention only of the dead. Then, in all their litanies, hymns, and proses where every kind of honor is paid to dead saints, there is no mention of Christ."[17]

Calvin's confusion here is rampant. First, he makes the mistake of assuming that by asking for the intercession of the saints, Catholics "reject the kindness of God" and, thereby, no longer have Christ as a brother (and by implication, as Lord and Savior). This charge is baseless, as we have seen above. For if asking a fellow Christian to pray for us constitutes "rejecting God's kindness," then clearly no Christian could have Christ as his brother, since all Christians, at least ostensibly, seek the prayers of fellow Christians.

By the way, a Catholic could respond wryly to

[17] *Institutes.*

Calvin with the words of St. Cyprian of Carthage:

> "You cannot have God as a father, unless you have the *Church* as mother."[18]

Back to Calvin. Notice how his argument distorts the Catholic teaching that was, even in his day, clearly enunciated: The intercession of Mary and the saints does not "replace" nor in any way is comparable in kind or degree to Christ's unique mediatorship. All Christians enter into the mystery of Christ's redemptive suffering, as St. Paul reminds us in Colossians 1:24-29, but always and only in a subordinate way to Christ. In his *Summa Theologiae*, St. Thomas Aquinas declared unequivocally:

> "Properly speaking, the office of a mediator is to join together and unite those between whom he mediates: for extremes are united in the mean (*media*). Now to unite men to God perfectly belongs to Christ, through Whom men are reconciled to God, according to 2 Cor. 5:19 — God was in Christ reconciling the world to Himself. And, consequently, *Christ alone is the perfect Mediator of God and men*, inasmuch as, by His death, He reconciled the human race to God."[19]

Had Calvin done his homework, he would have found an abundance of official Catholic teachings that Christ is the one Mediator and that no saint could possibly usurp this role.[20] Also, either

---

[18] "*Habere iam non potest Deum Patrem qui ecclesiam non habet matrem*" (*On the Unity of the Catholic Church* 5:7 [A.D. 251]).

[19] III, Q. 26, ad. 1.; cf. III, Q. 1, 2 ad. 2; Augustine, *Enarrationes in Psalmos*, 95:5.

[20] Eg. Pope St. Leo the Great, *Epistle to Flavian*, 3 (A.D.

deliberately or out of ignorance, he misrepresents the Catholic teaching on *why* we invoke the intercession of the saints when he writes:

> "[It is] the extreme of stupidity, not to say madness, to attempt to obtain access by means of others, so as to be drawn away from him without whom access cannot be obtained."[21]

Here again, Calvin argues in circles, for asking another Christian for prayer is not being "drawn away" from Christ. It does not entail an effort to "obtain access" in some creative way that allows us to ignore or circumvent Christ. Asking a fellow Christian for prayer in no way means that we see Christ's mediation as substandard. We'll develop in greater detail our biblical refutation of Calvin and the other Reformers shortly, but for the moment, let's remember that these statements of rejection show us that the various Reformation theologies all had one thing in common — an ecclesiology that was *radically* different from that of the Catholic ecclesiology that had preceded it for fifteen centuries.

By accusing this Catholic teaching[22] of being "the extreme of stupidity, not to say madness," Calvin and his Evangelical descendants are also charging St. Augustine, St. Cyril of Jerusalem (d. 386), St. John Chrysostom, the great Cappadocian Fathers, St.

---

449); Pope John IV, *Dominus Qui Dixit* (641), Pope St. Nicholas I, *Proposueramus Quidem* (865); Council of Florence, *Cantata Domino* (1442).

[21] Ibid.

[22] As well as other related Catholic doctrines like offering prayers for the repose of the souls of deceased Christians, purgatory, venerating relics, etc.

Basil of Caesarea (d. 379), St. Gregory Nazianzus (d. 390), and St. Gregory of Nyssa (d. 394) — indeed, the entire early Christian Church — as engaging in "the extreme of stupidity, not to say madness," for these eminent Fathers, too, held and taught this Catholic doctrine.[23]

In virtually all respects, the "gospel according to Protestantism" bears little resemblance to that of the early Christian Church. One of the most striking examples of this disparity is found in the issue of the communion of saints.

Protestants, especially Evangelicals and Fundamentalists, have at best a hazy knowledge of Church history. Most are not familiar at all with the early Church and, as a result, are startled to discover that the teaching of the Catholic Church regarding the communion of saints is identical with what the early Christians believed. The reason for the continuity? Because the early Christians were Catholic.

---

[23] Cf. William A. Jurgens, *Faith of the Early Fathers* (Collegeville: The Liturgical Press, 1970), for an extensive series of citations by these and other early Fathers on various Marian doctrines. Cf. Cyril of Jerusalem, *Catechetical Lectures*, 5:9.

Three

"Me and Jesus" Christianity Isn't Biblical

ST. PAUL SAID, "We . . . are one body in Christ and individually parts of one another" (Rom. 12:5). Catholics believe membership in Christ's Body means a personal relationship with Jesus and, through Him, with all Christians.

Although Protestants may agree with this in theory, in application most of them (this is especially true of Evangelicals and Fundamentalists) promote an individualistic "me and Jesus" version of Christianity, teaching that the only thing ultimately important is one's own relationship with Christ, independent of any relationship to anyone else. While it may pay lip service to the communion of saints, in reality most of Protestantism ignores the organic bond of unity between the Christian faithful, a bond which perdures beyond death.

Since Evangelicals and Fundamentalists follow the Catholic Church's teaching that the Bible is God's inspired, inerrant Word[24] (some Protestants, unfortunately, believe it is neither), the Bible is our common ground for dialogue. To be effective in explaining the communion. of saints to Protestants, Catholics must know how to present the biblical foundations of the doctrine.

Some Protestants will remain unmoved in their objections to this doctrine even in the face of a thoroughgoing biblical defense. But look closely and you'll see that what the Protestant really disagrees with is the Catholic *interpretation* of verses, thus moving the argument beyond the "It's not in the Bible" category to the purely subjective "I don't agree with your interpretation of these verses" category.

This attitude stems from Protestantism's fatal flaw, *sola scriptura*, the notion that the Bible is the sole infallible rule of faith, independent of Sacred Tradition or the magisterium. The scope of this work doesn't permit a detailed critique of *sola scriptura*[25], but it's sufficient to say the idea of the Bible alone, as propounded by the classical Protestant creeds is: a) unbiblical (ie. it is not found implicitly or explicitly

---

[24] Cf. *Dei Verbum* 9-10.

[25] For an exhaustive Catholic critique of *sola scriptura*, including detailed refutations based on history, scriptural exegesis, patristic testimony, and philosophical grounds, see Robert Sungenis, Patrick Madrid, et al., *Not By Scripture Alone* (Santa Barbara: Queenship Publishing, 1998).

taught anywhere in Scripture), b) unhistorical (ie. it was not a position taught by the early Church Fathers, nor was it practiced by the early Christians), and c) unworkable (ie. *sola scriptura,* as a principle of arriving at a correct understanding of Scripture, is a failure).

The sheer number of Protestant sects and denominations, and their myriads of conflicting opinions on the meaning of Scripture — especially as pertains to essential doctrinal issues — is ample proof that going by the Bible alone is a recipe for doctrinal catastrophe.

Typical Protestants demand that Catholics substantiate their beliefs in Scripture (the old "show me where it says that in the Bible" routine), yet when the demanded biblical evidence is produced, the Catholic conclusion is nonetheless rejected as "unscriptural." Since they reject the concept of an infallible interpreter of Scripture, whether it be the Church or an individual, Protestants can only put forth their own opinions on what they think Scripture means. They have no way of knowing for certain if their interpretation of the Bible is correct.

So let's outline the Catholic teaching on the communion of saints. The first step is to see that it rests on four pillars: (1) The Church is Christ's Body; (2) Christ has only one Body, not one on earth and one in heaven; (3) Christians are not separated from each other by death; (4) Christians must love and serve each other.

The Church Is Christ's Body

St. Paul's use of the body as an image to describe the unity Christians have with Christ and each other is particularly vivid: "For as in one body we have many parts, and all the parts do not have the same function, so we, though many, are one body in Christ and *individually parts of one another*" (Rom. 12:4-5).[26]

This passage, especially the last phrase — individually parts of one another — is the bedrock of the entire Catholic teaching on the communion of saints. It is because of our unity with Christ that we enjoy a real, organic unity with all other members of the Body of Christ. This biblical evidence is one of the clearest indictments of Protestantism's concept of the communion of saints. Catholics should take every opportunity to share the meaning of Romans 12 with their Protestant friends and ask how it is that, if we are "parts of one another," that Christians in heaven are somehow exempt from this teaching.

But unity between Christians is not something that only St. Paul spoke of. The Lord Himself alluded to this unity when He prayed, "May [they] be one, as we are one, I in them and You in Me, that they may be brought to perfection as one" (John 17:22-23). He used the analogy of Himself as a vine and Christians as its branches to illustrate the organic bond Christians share (John 15:1- 5).

The teaching that the Church is Christ's Body is

---

[26] Cf. CCC 787-795.

emphasized throughout the New Testament, most commonly in St. Paul's epistles.[27] But perhaps the most forceful identification of the Church with Christ comes from our Lord Himself, when He confronted Saul on the Road to Damascus:

> "Now Saul, still breathing murderous threats against the disciples of the Lord, went to the high priest and asked him for letters to the synagogues in Damascus, that, if he should find any men or women who belonged to the Way, he might bring them back to Jerusalem in chains. On his journey, as he was nearing Damascus, a light from the sky suddenly flashed around him. He fell to the ground and heard a voice saying to him, 'Saul, Saul, why are you persecuting *me?*' He said, 'Who are you, Sir?' The reply came, '*I am Jesus, whom you are persecuting*'" (Acts 9:1-5).[28]

This passage clearly identifies the nature of the Church as being Christ Himself. Understanding this key biblical truth — the real connection between Christ and the Church — is the foundation to everything we'll see after this.

Christ Has Only One Body

Jesus has only one Body — not one on earth and another one in heaven. St. Paul emphasized this when he wrote:

> "But now in Christ Jesus you who once were far

---

[27] Cf. 1 Cor. 10:16, 12:12-27; Gal. 3:28; Eph. 1:22-23, 3:4-6, 4:4,15, 25, 5:21-32; Col. 1:18, 3:15; Heb. 13:1-3.

[28] Cf. Augustine, *City of God* 17:9; Cyprian, *On the Glory of Martyrdom* 3.

off have been brought near in the blood of Christ. For He is our peace, who has *made us both one*, and has broken down the dividing wall of hostility, by abolishing in His flesh the law of commandments and ordinances, that He might create in himself *one* new man in place of the two, so making peace, and might reconcile us both to God in *one body* through the cross, thereby bringing the hostility to an end" (Eph. 2:13-16).[29]

He also wrote:

"For as many of you as were baptized into Christ have put on Christ. There is neither Jew nor Greek, there is neither slave nor free, there is neither male nor female; for *you are all one in Christ Jesus*" (Gal. 3:27-28).

St. Paul also made use of the image of a house to stress the unity in Christ of all believers, linking it to the concept of living together in one house:

"I hope to come to you soon, but I am writing these instructions to you so that, if I am delayed, you may know how one ought to behave in the household of God, which is the church of the living God, the pillar and foundation of the truth" (1 Tim. 3:14-15).

Christ Himself spoke often of this mystical unity that all Christians would enjoy through union with Him.[30]

"I do not pray for these only, but also for those who believe in me through their word, that they may all be one; even as thou, Father, art in me,

---

[29] Cf. Rom. 12:4-5; 1 Cor. 10:17, 12:12-27; Eph. 4:4-5, Col. 3:14-15.

[30] Eg. John 10:16, 15:1-7, 17:11.

and I in thee, that they also may be in us, so that the world may believe that thou hast sent me. The glory which thou hast given me I have given to them, that they may be one even as we are one, I in them and thou in me, that they may become perfectly one" (John 17:20-22).

Catholics, taking Christ at His word, believe what the Bible says. All Christians, including those in heaven, are members of that one Body of Christ. This unity is, in fact, one of the four "marks of the Church." The Nicene Creed includes as part of its list of essential beliefs for early Christians, the phrase, "I believe . . . in *one*, holy, catholic, and apostolic Church."[31] It's upon the concept of "oneness" that the reality of the communion of saints rests.

The early Christians had a clear understanding that this Catholic "oneness" of believers included Christians who had died and gone to heaven, as well as those who are being detained for a time in purgatory. This is most clearly manifested in the early liturgies of the Christian Church. These liturgies abound with commemorations of the departed saints, especially the martyrs, and there is a consistent and pervasive practice among the early Christians of asking Mary and the saints to intercede for Christians on earth. They are a powerful testimony regarding how attentive the early Church was in asking for the intercessory prayers of Mary and the saints, as well as in offering propitiatory prayers on behalf of the dead in Christ (ie. those in purgatory).

---

[31] "*Credo in unum Deum . . . et unam, sanctam, catholicam et apostolicam Ecclesiam.*"

One such liturgy, the Divine Liturgy of the Holy Apostle and Evangelist Mark, contains this prayer:

> "Give peace, O sovereign Lord our God, to the souls of all who dwell in the tabernacles of the saints . . . Give peace to their souls and deem them worthy of the kingdom of heaven."[32]

The early Church was intensely conscious of the reality of the communion of saints and relied heavily on the intercession of the Blessed Virgin Mary and the saints. The ancient Christian liturgies reveal a deep reverence for the bond of unity in Christ shared by all Christians, on earth, in purgatory, and in heaven. Understanding this is crucial to understanding the development of the Catholic Church's teaching on the communion of saints.[33]

The irony is that in spite of Protestantism's various anti-Catholic[34] objections to the fact that physical death does not destroy the unity of Christians (and all that that teaching entails), the creeds of Protestantism actually support the Catholic teaching, though implicitly. Classical Protestant confessional statements and writings by the Reformers

---

[32] Cf. *The Divine Liturgy of James*, Ante-Nicene Fathers (Peabody: Hendrickson, 1992 ed.), 7:537-550; cf., ibid. 7:556:15. For an exhaustive study of these and other ancient Christian liturgies, see Casimir Kucharek, *The Byzantine-Slav Liturgy of St. John Chrysostom* (Combermere, ONT: Alleluia Press: 1971).

[33] F. Bente and W. H. T. Dau, translators, *Triglot Concordia: The Symbolical Books of the Evangelical Lutheran Church* [St. Louis: Concordia Publishing House, 1921], 453-529).

[34] I use "anti-Catholic" here not in the emotional, pejorative sense, but in the sense of opposing this Catholic doctrine on theological and biblical grounds.

actually recognize this Catholic principle, though they don't admit it explicitly. In 1537 Luther described membership in the Church this way:

> "We do not concede to them [the Catholics] that they are the Church, and they are not [the true Church]; nor will we listen to those things which, under the name of Church, they enjoin or forbid. For, thank God, [today] a child seven years old knows what the Church is, namely, *the holy believers and lambs who hear the voice of their Shepherd.* For the children pray thus: I believe in one holy [catholic or] Christian Church. This holiness does not consist in albs, tonsures, long gowns, and other of their ceremonies devised by them beyond Holy Scripture, but in the Word of God and true faith."[35]

The implication of Luther's admission that (at the very least) membership in the Church consists in being one of "the holy believers and lambs who hear the voice of their Shepherd" is clear: Mary and the saints in heaven thereby qualify *par excellence* as "holy believers" (cf. Rev. 5:8, 8:2-4). But this means that if they are members in the Body of Christ, their ongoing *participation* in the Body of Christ is a fact. And this is exactly where the Catholic teaching on the communion of saints becomes bothersome to Protestants.

An Evangelical Protestant might be willing to say the saints in heaven are members of the Body of Christ, but he will refuse to acknowledge that they are capable of or permitted to *do* anything by way of interacting with members of the Body who are still

---

[35] *Smalcald Articles*, chapter 12.

on earth. The reasons they object to this will be given later in this book, but for now, let's consider the other things the Bible tells us about the nature of the Church and the relationship all Christians — in heaven and on earth — have to Christ and, through Him, with each other.

Death Does Not Separate Christians

Because of Christ's victory over death, a victory in which all Christians share,[36] mere physical death can't separate Christians from Christ or from each other. That's why Paul exulted,

> "What will separate us from the love of Christ?... I am convinced that neither death, nor life . . . will be able to separate us from the love of God in Jesus Christ our Lord" (Rom. 8:35-39).

Some Protestants argue that this passage does not entail the Catholic claim that death doesn't separate Christians. But that's not true.[37]

Let's look at this text closely. When Paul says "the love of Christ" he's referring to more than just Christ's love for His people. After all, to be in Christ's

---

[36] Cf. 1 Cor. 15:25-26, 54-56; 2 Cor. 2:14; 2 Tim. 1:10.

[37] Ironically, the classical Protestant creeds and the writings of the Reformers reveal that Protestantism in its various forms does in fact recognize the fact that death does not sever the bond of unity between believers here on earth and those who now enjoy the Beatific Vision. The *Westminster Confession*, for example, declares, "The catholic or universal church, which is invisible, consists of the *whole number of the elect*, that have been, are, or shall be gathered into one, under Christ the head thereof" (27:1); emphasis added.

love means to be in Christ himself — i.e., in His Body, the Church.[38] Those who are "in Christ" are inseparable from Him so long as they don't voluntarily choose to separate from Him.[39]

Since death has no power to sever the bond of Christian unity, the relationship between Christians on earth and those in heaven remains intact. Therefore, when we read biblical passages about how members of the Body of Christ need each other or are obligated to assist and pray for one another, Catholics recognize that they apply to Christians in heaven, too.

The Protestant animus against the idea that saints in heaven can or should pray for us stems from an "out of sight, out of mind" mentality: "Since I no longer can see and speak to departed Christians, they must no longer matter to me." This myopic position is not only not scriptural, it actually clashes with verses that Protestants know by heart. For example, St. Paul chides Christians who think they don't need other Christians:

> "God placed the parts, each one of them, in the body as He intended. If they were all one part, where would the body be? But as it is, there are many parts, yet one body. *The eye cannot say to the hand, 'I do not need you,' nor again the head [say] to the feet, 'I do not need you.'* . . . God has so constructed the body as to give greater honor to a part that is without it, so that there may be no division in the body, but that the parts may have the

---

[38] Cf. Rom. 8:1-2.
[39] Cf. Matt. 18:23-35; 1 Cor. 9:27; Rom. 11:22-23; Heb. 10:26-31.

same concern for one another. If one part suffers, all the parts suffer with it; if one part is honored, all the parts share its joy."[40]

The theological implications of this passage are enormous: *"The eye cannot say to the hand, 'I do not need you,' nor again the head [say] to the feet, 'I do not need you.'"* Every Catholic should engrave this verse (among others) on his heart and be able to quote it from memory when faced with a Protestant attack on the communion of saints. The Catholic should explain how death cannot separates Christians, nor can it sever their organic unity in Christ. Then he should ask the Protestant to explain St. Paul's teaching that no member of the Body of Christ can say, "I do not need you" to another member. You can't get around it.

Where Does the Bible Talk About It?

As we've seen above in the few representative citations from the Reformation creeds and polemical writings, the charge is always leveled: "The Bible nowhere mentions (much less endorses) the idea that saints can pray for us. So how does the Catholic Church justify its claim that we should ask Mary and the saints for their prayers?"

First, remember that the Protestant notion of *sola scriptura* is itself an unbiblical "tradition of men"[41] and is not what the early Church practiced. Therefore, the Catholic should respond to this

---

[40] 1 Cor. 12:18-20, 24-26.
[41] Cf. Mark 7:7-8; Matt. 15:1-9.

challenge first by explaining that, biblically speaking, the Bible doesn't *have* to command that a certain thing be done; and second, that the Bible doesn't need to even mention in a positive way that it was done at all.[42] Even so, there is Biblical evidence for the intercession of the saints (though from a book rejected by Protestants). Here's one example of a departed saint interceding for those still living on earth:

> "But Maccabeus did not cease to trust with all confidence that he would get help from the Lord. And he exhorted his men not to fear the attack of the Gentiles, but to keep in mind the former times when help had come to them from heaven, and now to look for the victory which the Almighty would give them. Encouraging them from the law and the prophets, and reminding them also of the struggles they had won, he made them the more eager. And when he had aroused their courage, he gave his orders, at the same time pointing out the perfidy of the Gentiles and their violation of oaths. He armed each of them not so much with confidence in shields and spears as with the inspiration of brave words, and he cheered them all by relating a dream, a sort of vision, which was worthy of belief.

> "What he saw was this: Onias, who had been high priest, a noble and good man, of modest bearing and gentle manner, one who spoke fittingly and had been trained from childhood in all that

---

[42] Protestants will resist this answer, of course. That means that Catholics should know the biblical and historical case against *sola scriptura* and be able to explain why the "Bible only" approach is itself unbiblical.

belongs to excellence, *was praying with out-stretched hands for the whole body of the Jews.* Then likewise a man appeared, distinguished by his gray hair and dignity, and of marvelous majesty and authority. And Onias spoke, saying, *'This is a man who loves the brethren and prays much for the people and the holy city, Jeremiah, the prophet of God.'* Jeremiah stretched out his right hand and gave to Judas a golden sword, and as he gave it he addressed him thus: 'Take this holy sword, a gift from God, with which you will strike down your adversaries.'"[43]

Since this passage comes from one of the seven deuterocanonical books of the Bible eliminated by Martin Luther (and subsequently rejected by virtually all of Protestantism), it will be unacceptable to an Evangelical as biblical proof. Nonetheless, Catholics should be aware of such explicit biblical texts regarding the issue of the saints being able to pray and intercede for us (Protestant objections notwithstanding).[44]

Christians Are United in Charity

The fourth pillar in the communion of saints framework is Christ's law of charity. Jesus said that loving one another is second in importance only to loving God (Matt. 22:38, Mark 12:30-31, 1 Cor. 13).

This law of charity is emphasized in the New

---

[43] 2 Macc. 15:7-16.
[44] Protestant objections to these books are answered by Mark Shea in "Five Myths About Seven Books," March/April 1997 (*Envoy* Magazine, New Hope, KY 40052, 800-55-ENVOY, www.envoymagazine.com).

Testament at every turn, especially in the form of intercessory prayer. Paul exhorts Christians to pray, supplicate, petition, and intercede for all people. He emphasizes that intercessory prayer "is *good and pleasing to God our savior*" (1 Tim. 2:1-4). Similar exhortations permeate the New Testament:

> "I urge you, brothers, by our Lord Jesus Christ and by the love of the Spirit, to join me in the struggle by your prayers to God on my behalf" (Rom. 15:30-32).

> "In Him we have put our hope that He will also rescue us again, as you help us with prayer" (2 Cor. 1:10).

> "We always give thanks to God, the Father of our Lord Jesus Christ, when we pray for you . . . we do not cease praying for you and asking that you may be filled with the knowledge of His will through all spiritual wisdom and understanding to live in a manner worthy of the Lord" (Col. 1:4, 9-10).[45]

If, while on earth, St. Paul could say, "My heart's desire and prayer to God on their behalf is for salvation" (Rom. 10:1) and "I remember you constantly in my prayers, night and day. I yearn to see you again" (2 Tim. 1:3), is there any reason to imagine that upon entering heaven Paul's charity and desire for others' salvation would be quenched and his prayers for others cease? Not at all. The Bible's

---

[45] Cf. Acts 8:24; 2 Cor. 13:7; Phil. 1:9; Gal. 5:13, 6:2; Eph. 4:32; 1 Thess. 3:10-12, 4:9-18, 5:14-15, 25; 2 Thess. 1:3, 3:1; 1 Tim. 2:14; 2 Tim. 1:34; Heb. 3:19,13:18; Jas. 5:16-18; 1 Pet. 1:22, 3:8; 1 John 4:7-21; 2 John 5.

many exhortations to mutual charity apply to *all* Christians, so they must apply to Christians in heaven. Consider these admonitions:

> "Bear one anothers' burdens, and so you will fulfill the law of Christ" (Gal. 6:2).

> "Love one another with mutual affection; anticipate one another in showing honor. . . contribute to the needs of the saints" (Rom. 12:9-10).

> "No one should seek his own advantage, but that of his neighbor" (1 Cor. 10:24).

> "On the subject of mutual charity you have no need for anyone to write you, for you yourselves have been taught by God to love one another. . . Nevertheless, we urge you, brothers, to progress even more" (1 Thess. 4:9-10).

> "Encourage one another, and build one another up . . . We urge you, brothers, admonish the idle, cheer the fainthearted, support the weak . . . always seek what is good both for each other and for all" (1 Thess. 5:11, 14-15; cf. 2 Cor. 1:10-11).

Examples of these New Testament exhortations to charity could be multiplied, but the point is this: Christ's law of love is a *standing command* for His Church. It doesn't matter whether a Christian is living here on earth or living in heavenly glory in the immediate presence of the Lord; he is still bound under Christ's command to "love one another."

Four

The "One Mediator" Argument and Other Common Objections

OF ALL THE VARIOUS Protestant objections to the communion of saints, the most common is the "one mediator" argument. As we saw, Calvin and other Reformers appealed to this passage in their attack on the Catholic doctrine of the communion of saints, so it's important that we examine it and related passages carefully:

"For there is one God, and there is one mediator between God and men, the man Christ Jesus" (1 Tim. 2:5).

Pinning their hopes on the strength of this verse, Protestants argue that since Christ is the one mediator between God and men, asking Mary and the saints in heaven to intercede for us constitutes a gross infringement on His unique role. "This shouldn't be done!" they say. "We should just pray to God directly, period."

Actually, Catholics do both and, ironically, so do Protestants. This is a concept that, if explained biblically, most Protestants will understand and agree with. Catholics and Protestants both pray directly to God and also ask their fellow Christians to pray for them. The difference is that Catholics don't restrict the term "Christians" to mean "only Christians on earth."

It must be made very clear that the Catholic Church in no way teaches that the saints are mediators in the special sense used in 1 Timothy 2:5.[46] Protestants worry that Catholics are trying to usurp the unique role of Christ as the one mediator and transfer that role to Mary and the saints.

But this is not at all what the Catholic Church teaches, and we Catholics need to make every effort to make that clear to Protestants. Let's look at what the Catholic Church teaches about Christ's mediatorship.

First, because of the Incarnation, Christ has an absolutely unique role as mediator. Since He is the only one Who is God and man,[47] the only contact point between us and the Father, only He is capable

---

[46] Cf. CCC 618, 1544, 2574, 2634.

[47] Protestant scholar Dieter Sanger's aphorism hits the nail on the head: "He is the one who represents God to mankind and mankind to God" (article on μεσιτης [mesites] in Balz & Schneider, eds., Exegetical Dictionary of the New Testament [Grand Rapids: Eerdmans, 1991], 2:411). Cf. CCC 613-618.

of bridging the chasm of sin that separates us from God.

> "Intercession is a prayer of petition which leads us to pray as Jesus did. He is the one intercessor with the father on behalf of all men, especially sinners (cf. Rom. 8:34; 1 John 2:1; 1 Tim. 2:5-8). He is 'able for all time to save those who draw near to God through Him, since He always lives to make intercession for them' (Heb. 7:25)."[48]

Clearly, no saint can usurp Christ's role as the one mediator. Nor does the Catholic Church teach that any Christian is a mediator in the sense used in 1 Timothy 2:5 regarding Christ. It teaches, as the Bible does, that all Christians are *intercessors* who, because of Christ's mediatorship, are able to pray for each other.[49]

> "Since Abraham (cf. Gen. 18:16-23), intercession — asking on behalf of another — has been characteristic of a heart attuned to God's mercy. In the age of the Church, Christian intercession participates in Christ's, as an expression of the communion of saints. In intercession, he who prays looks 'not only to his own interests, but also to the interests of others,' even to the point of praying for those who do him harm."[50]

The episode the *Catechism* refers to here is where Abraham, aware that God planned to destroy

---

[48] CCC 2634 (cf. 1037, 1900, 2571, 2577).

[49] The official Catholic position on this issue was defined at the Council of Trent, Session 5 ("Decree on Original Sin"), and in Session 25 ("Decree on the Invocation of Saints").

[50] CCC 2635.

Sodom and Gomorrah because of their sins and blasphemies, interceded with God on behalf of the inhabitants of those wicked cities. Notice that he intercedes for the good and bad alike, asking God to spare these cities for the sake of the just people He might find there:

> "Then Abraham drew near, and said, 'Wilt thou indeed destroy the righteous with the wicked? Suppose there are fifty righteous within the city; wilt thou then destroy the place and not spare it for the fifty righteous who are in it?' . . . And the Lord said, 'If I find at Sodom fifty righteous in the city, I will spare the whole place for their sake.' Abraham answered, 'Behold, I have taken upon myself to speak to the Lord, I who am but dust and ashes. Suppose five of the fifty righteous are lacking? Wilt thou destroy the whole city for lack of five?' And He said, 'I will not destroy it if I find forty-five there'" (Gen. 18:23-28).

The conversation ensued to the point where Abraham had reduced the number to ten, and the Lord agreed not to carry out His plan to destroy the cities for the sake of those ten. This biblical example sheds light on the Catholic doctrine of the communion of saints.

This exchange shows a two-fold merit: Abraham's (God listened to Abraham's prayer and agreed to grant his petition precisely because of Abraham's own righteousness) and that of the "righteous men" Abraham hoped God would find there. God was willing to spare the cities for their sake. This is a clear example of a friend of God interceding for others (even those who don't deserve it) and God is willing to grant the request because of the merit of the one who intercedes.

Second, this passage shows us that God's friends are moved by charity for their neighbor and actively seek their well-being. Abraham's intercession for others is a perfect biblical model of how all the saints see us. Because they love God, they have grown to become like God. This means they go out of their way to show charity, to look for ways to help others, to plead for mercy on behalf of others, even those who don't deserve it.

We see this principle of meritorious intercessory prayer in various places in the Old Testament, but perhaps most striking in the book of Job:

> "And it came to pass after the Lord had spoken these words to Job, that the Lord said to Eliphaz the Temanite: 'I am angry with you and with your two friends; for you have not spoken rightly concerning me, as has my servant Job. Now, therefore, take seven bulls and seven rams, and go to my servant Job, and offer up for a holocaust for yourselves; and let my servant Job pray for you, *for his prayer I will accept*, not to punish you severely; for you have not spoken rightly concerning me, as has my servant Job.' Then Eliphaz the Temanite and Bildad the Shuhite and Zophar the Naamathite went and did as the Lord had commanded them. And *the Lord accepted the intercession of Job*. Also, the Lord restored the prosperity of Job, after he had prayed for his friends; the Lord even gave to Job twice as much as he had before."[51]

This biblical principle of interceding for others in

---

[51] Job 42:7-10.

prayer is perfectly reasonable to a Protestant. If asked whether he has objections to one Christian praying for another, he'll say no. So remind him that asking Christians in heaven to pray for us is essentially the same thing as asking a Christian here on earth to do so.

If he won't go along with this line of reasoning, point out that if asking Christians in heaven to pray for us conflicts with Christ's mediatorship, asking Christians on *earth* to pray for us conflicts for the same reason. If 1 Timothy 2:5 eliminates intercession by the Christians in heaven, it eliminates intercession by Christians on earth.

But this would be a serious misreading of the text. Far from excluding Christians from a share in Christ's mediatorship, Paul is actually emphasizing that we share in it through intercessory prayers. Our intercessions are effectual precisely and only because Christ is the one mediator.

"Mini-Mediators"

When he commanded that "supplications, prayers, petitions, and thanksgivings be offered for everyone . . . for this is good and pleasing to God our savior" (1 Tim. 2:1,3), St. Paul was calling all Christians to exercise a "mini-mediatorship" through and in Christ. After all, someone who prays, supplicates, and petitions is a go-between — a mediator who goes to God on behalf of someone else, interceding for him and asking the Lord to grant that person blessings or healing or strength or forgiveness or salvation. This is exactly what we saw Abraham doing in Genesis 18.

But we must remember that Christian mediatorship through intercessory prayer is qualitatively different from the mediatorship of Jesus, and it's only possible because Jesus Christ is the one mediator between us and the Father. Because of His death on the cross, we can now go boldly into the presence of the Father and pray, intercede, petition, and supplicate on behalf of others.

"And He came and preached peace to you who were far off and peace to those who were near; for through Him we both have access in one Spirit to the Father. So then you are no longer strangers and sojourners, but you are fellow citizens with the saints and members of the household of God" (Eph. 2:17-19; cf. 1 Tim. 2:1-4, Heb. 4:16).

Another reason there's no conflict between asking fellow Christians for prayers and believing that Jesus is the one mediator between God and man is that Jesus shares His other unique roles in lesser ways with Christians. Here are several examples of this truth:

Jesus is the *creator* of all things (John 1:1-3, Col. 1:16-17, Heb. 1:1-2), yet when it comes to creating human life, He shares this role with men and women, mediating His creatorship through us via sexual intercourse. The human soul is created by God, out of nothing, at the instant the marital union produces a new body. The Lord could have chosen to create human life, body and soul, directly and unilaterally, but He didn't, preferring instead to make His role as Creator dependent in a way on human action.

Jesus is the *shepherd* of His flock, the Church (John 10:16), yet He shares His shepherdhood in a subordinate way with others, beginning with Peter (John 21:15-17) and extending it later to others (Eph. 4:11).[52] The apostles and their successors, the bishops, are truly shepherds also.

Jesus is the *high priest* of the New Covenant, eternally present before the Father, mediating His once-for-all sacrifice for our redemption (Heb. 3:1, 4:14-15, 5:5-10, 7:15-26, 8:1, 9:11). But the Bible also says that all Christians are called to share in Christ's priesthood (1 Pet. 2:4-5, 5-9; Rev. 1:6, 5:10, 20:6).

Jesus is the *supreme judge* (John 5:27, 9:39; Rom. 14:10; 2 Cor. 5:10; 2 Tim 4:1), yet Christians are called to share in Christ's judgeship. They will be judges in heaven, even judging the angels (Matt. 19:28; Luke 22:30; 1 Cor. 6:2-3; Rev. 20:4).

Jesus is the *sovereign king* of the universe (Mark 15:32; 1 Tim. 1:17, 6:15; Rev. 15:3,17:14, 19:16), but He shares His kingship with all Christians, who in

---

[52] After saying He's the Good Shepherd, Jesus says He's the *only* shepherd (John 10:11-16), yet this seemingly exclusive statement doesn't conflict with Him making Peter shepherd over the flock (John 21:15-17) or with His calling others to be shepherds as well (Eph. 4:11). Peter emphasizes that Jesus shares His role as shepherd with others by calling Jesus the Chief Shepherd, thus implying lesser shepherds (1 Pet. 5:4). Note also that the Greek construction of John 10:16 ([there is] one shepherd, [*heis poimen*] is the same as 1 Timothy 2:5: [there is] one mediator [*heis mesites*].

heaven will wear crowns, sit on thrones, and reign as kings alongside Jesus (Rev. 4:4,10) — but who will always be subordinate to Him. Notice the promises the Lord makes:

> "I will give the victor the right to sit with me on my throne, as I myself first won the victory and sit with my Father on His throne" (Rev. 3:21).

> "Truly, I say to you, in the new world, when the Son of man shall sit on His glorious throne, you who have followed me will also sit on twelve thrones, judging the twelve tribes of Israel" (Matt. 19:28).

Scripture also depicts the Blessed Virgin Mary herself in royal glory in heaven:

> "And a great sign appeared in heaven, a woman clothed with the sun, with the moon under her feet, and on her head a crown of twelve stars" (Rev. 12:1).[53]

We see similar passages describing God's plan to share His kingship with His friends throughout Scripture (cf. 1 Sam. 2:8; Luke 22:28-30; 2 Tim. 2:12; Rev. 1:6, 5:10).

Jesus is the *divine physician* — the one Who forgives our sins, heals our spiritual infirmities, and

---

[53] Although some scholars hold that the "woman" glimpsed in Revelation 12:1 is the Church or Israel, I favor the interpretation that it is Mary. For a popular analysis of this exegesis, see John Henry Newman, *Mary, the Second Eve* (Rockford: TAN Books and Publishers, 1990); it provides an excellent biblical discussion of the Marian interpretation of this passage and shows this view as held by the early Church Fathers.

reconciles us to the Father and to the Church (cf. 2 Cor. 5:18-21), but Jesus also calls us to share in various ways in His ministry of forgiveness and reconciliation.[54] The mission of Christ to reconcile the world to the Father is carried out in many ways through us. After all, Christ does not personally appear to people and urge them to repent of their sins. Nor does He personally baptize them. These ministries of reconciliation have been entrusted to the Church,[55] yet this fact in no way jeopardizes or minimizes the fact that Christ is *the* minister of forgiveness and reconciliation between ourselves and the Father.

Clearly, no Christian can usurp Christ's unique roles as creator, shepherd, priest, king, judge, and reconciler, but each Christian is called to share in these roles in subordinate ways. The principle of sharing in Christ's roles extends, in the form of intercessory prayer, to Christ's mediatorship, as well.

Praying Straight to God?

Another common argument against prayers to saints is, "Why pray to the saints when you can go straight to God?"

Protestants argue that verses such as these imply we should go only to God for our needs: "Through [Jesus] we both have access in one Spirit to the Father" (Eph. 2:18); "Let us confidently

---

[54] Cf. Matt. 9:5-8, 18:18; John 20:21-22; Acts 2:38; 2 Cor. 5:18-20; James 5:14-15.
[55] Cf. John 20:21.

approach the throne of grace to receive mercy and to find grace for timely help" (Heb. 4:16); "We have one who speaks to the Father in our defense, Jesus Christ, the righteous one" (1 John 2:1). They feel that asking the saints for prayer is superfluous since, through Jesus, we now have a direct line to God. No "helpers" are necessary.

Sometimes this argument takes the form of an analogy: "If you had complete, unrestricted access to the President of the United States and could see him whenever you had a complaint or needed a favor, why waste your time going to see the Secretary of State or the Chief of Staff when you could go directly into the Oval Office and get what you want from the man who makes the decisions?"

In other words, why ask the saints to pester God for you (as though they can convince Him to do things and you can't), when God loves you and wants to give you good things if you just ask Him?

Although this analogy is superficially reasonable, in reality this is an incredibly obtuse line of reasoning.

Of course God wants us to ask Him for things directly — and we do — but He also wants us to ask each other for prayers (cf. 1 Tim. 2:1-3). What Protestant, when asked for prayer by a fellow Christian, would whirl on his heel and snarl, "How unbiblical! Why would you ask *me* to pray for you, when you can go directly to God and ask Him yourself?" Protestants realize that sharing in Christ's mediatorship on earth by intercessory prayer is no more "unbiblical" than sharing in Christ's priesthood or kingship or judgeship.

In fact, many Protestants positively *delight* in being asked for intercessory prayer,[56] and they actively encourage it in others, especially in those they consider "prayer warriors," righteous Christians renowned for the efficacy of their prayers. James 5:16 says:

> "The fervent prayer of a righteous person is very powerful."

This passage in James points out what we have seen already in Scripture. In Genesis 18:22-32, we see a perfect example of intercessory prayer. Here God declares that He would be willing to grant Abraham's request for leniency for the wicked inhabitants of Sodom and Gomorrah. This passage shows that God was willing to grant this request on the basis of the righteousness of Abraham, who was interceding, and on the basis of the theoretical 50, 40, 30, 20, and 10 righteous inhabitants.

But we're concerned here with the issue of the saints in heaven — the righteous men and women who see God face-to-face, His intimate friends. They are vastly more righteous than even the holiest Christian on earth. Hebrews 12:22-24 says:

> "But you have come to Mount Zion and to the city of the living God, the heavenly Jerusalem, and to innumerable angels in festal gathering, and to the assembly of the first-born who are enrolled in heaven, and to a judge who is God of all, *and to the spirits of just men made perfect*, and to Jesus,

---

[56] Isn't it reasonable to imagine the saints are just as delighted when asked for their prayers?

the mediator of a new covenant, and to the sprinkled blood that speaks more graciously than the blood of Abel."

Christians in heaven have been "made perfect" in righteousness through the grace of Christ. Should their prayers be discounted? Of course not! To ignore their role as "prayer warriors" makes no scriptural sense. Catholics should become practiced at explaining these biblical truths to Protestants and ask, in light of what Scripture says about the power of the prayers of a righteous person, how they can ignore or deny the efficacy of prayers by the most righteous ones of all humanity, the blessed in heaven.

Jesus teaches that the saints are "put in charge of many things" in Matthew 25:21. This indicates that they have a service to perform for the Lord. Obviously, there is nothing to "take charge of" in heaven itself, since there, all is perfect bliss. Rather, they perform the charitable service of offering holy and pleasing "supplications, prayers, petitions, and thanksgivings" on behalf of their brothers and sisters on earth and in purgatory.

A Common Protestant Argument

Loraine Boettner, the godfather of modern anti-Catholicism, takes a different tack in his argument:

> "How dishonoring it is to Christ to teach that he is lacking in pity and compassion for his people and that he must be persuaded to that end . . . When he was on earth it was never necessary for

anyone to persuade him to be compassionate.[57] Rather, when he saw the blind and the lame, the afflicted and hungry, he was moved with compassion for them and lifted them out of their distress. He had immediate mercy on the wicked but penitent Thief on the cross, and there was no need for intercession by Mary although she was there present. His love for us is as great as when he was on earth; his heart is as tender; and we need no other intermediary, neither his mother after the flesh, nor any saint or angel, to entreat him on our behalf. Thus Christ, because he is both God and man, is the only Savior, the only Mediator, the only way to God. Not one word is said about Mary . . . or the saints as mediators. Yet Romanism teaches that there are many mediators."[58]

This is a feeble contrivance. Note that Boettner never really engages the Catholic position. He, like Calvin, argues against a straw man and not what the Catholic Church actually teaches. He insinuates that Catholics believe that God *needs* Mary or the saints to intercede for us or else He won't act. No Catholic believes it's "necessary" for anyone to

---

[57] This is untrue. There are a number of biblical cases in which Jesus was persuaded to be compassionate. A particularly striking example is the Canaanite woman who had to beg Jesus repeatedly for mercy (almost to the point of arguing with Him) before He would agree to cure her daughter (Matt. 15:21-28).

[58] *Roman Catholicism* (Philadelphia: Presbyterian and Reformed, 1962),147-148. Boettner's pseudo-scholarly brand of anti-Catholicism is widely used as a source for contemporary anti-Catholics. His arguments, though generally vapid, reflect a common approach used by Evangelicals and Fundamentalists and so they must be reckoned with.

persuade God about anything.

Boettner (and the host of modern Protestant apologists who have recycled his arguments) conveniently ignores the fact that the Bible says God is *pleased* by intercessory prayer (cf. 1 Tim. 2:14) and that sometimes, for His own inscrutable reasons, the Lord intervenes only as a result of the intercession by human beings. St. Paul emphasizes that God frequently grants gifts "through the prayers of many" (2 Cor. 1:10-11).

Boettner neglects to mention the biblical example of Mary's intercession with Christ in the relatively mundane matter of the wedding at Cana (John 2:1-10), nor does he deal with the fact that the martyrs in heaven intercede with God, beseeching Him to avenge their deaths (Rev. 6:9-11).

The Bible is full of examples of angels and saints interceding with God on behalf of others. Abraham intercedes on behalf of Sodom and Gomorrah (Gen. 18:16-32). Moses intercedes for the people of Israel, begging God not to destroy them, and God relents (Ex. 32:7-14). An angel intercedes on behalf of Jerusalem (Zech. 1:12). Paul intercedes on behalf of the Church (Col. 1:9-12).

Not All Prayer Is Worship

There is a more fundamental reason Protestants object to the invocation of saints. Many of them, especially Evangelicals and Fundamentalists, have a poor understanding of prayer.

Since the highest form of worship Protestants

have is prayer (they make no distinction between prayer and worship), Catholic prayers to saints seem blasphemous since we *pray* to saints. In fact, the highest form of worship is not prayer but the Mass — Christ's own once-for-all sacrifice on Calvary,[59] re-presented for us in space and time. There can be no other sacrifice than the one Christ offered on the Cross. Catholics should point out to Protestants that the sacrifice of the Mass is a real participation in that once-for-all sacrifice on Calvary.[60]

Although all worship is prayer, not all prayer is worship. Prayers to saints are no more worship than is asking a fellow Christian for prayer. There's no other way to ask those in heaven to intercede for us except by mental communication, and we call this communication "prayer," but it should not be confused with the prayer of worship given to God alone.

The "Multiple Prayers" Objection

There's also the "multiple prayer" objection: How can the saints hear all those millions of simultaneous prayers, in all those different languages? To be able to do that would require them to be omniscient and omnipresent, but only God is omniscient and omnipresent. One Protestant apologist argues that "To pray to Mary is to ascribe attributes of deity to her."[61] This is faulty reasoning on three levels.

---

[59] Cf. Heb. 7:27, 9:11-14, 23-28, 10:1-15.
[60] Cf. CCC 1330, 1357, 1359, 1364-1366.
[61] Eric Svendsen, *Protestant Answers: A Response to Recent Attacks Against Protestant Theology by Catholic Apologists* (Atlanta: New Testament Restoration Foundation Publi-

First, since the saints are living in eternity they aren't limited by time and space as we are, because they are beyond both. One might say it takes no time at all to hear all those prayers because the saints have no time.

Second, since no matter how many prayers might ascend to heaven in any given moment, there is still only a finite number of people on earth and, therefore, there would only be a finite number of prayers at any one time. So, neither omniscience nor omnipresence is required to hear all the prayers ever prayed at one time, no matter how great their number. (Remember that "omniscience" and "omnipresence," as divine attributes, refer to God's *infinite* knowledge and presence.)

Third, it's silly to think that the abilities of the saints in heaven are as paltry as ours. Our inability to understand *how* the saints can hear so many prayers is hardly a reason to deny that they *can* hear them. In their glorified state, the saints are capable of doing things we can barely imagine.

We know that in heaven we'll be transformed into the image of Christ's glorious, resurrected body. "We shall be like Him," Paul assures us (Phil. 3:20-21). John says, "We are God's children now; what we shall be has not yet been revealed. We do know that we shall be like Him, for we shall see Him as He is" (1 John 3:2).

In His resurrected, glorified body, Jesus did all sorts of incredible things, such as walk through walls (John 20:19). The wonderful thing is that the

cations, 1995), 92.

glory He had after the Resurrection is something promised to all of God's friends. While we may not understand the mechanics of how and in what measure these super-enhancements of human nature are bestowed by God, we know for sure that the saints in heaven do share in this unimaginable glory. The abilities and privileges, both spiritual and physical, the saints in heaven are graced with by Christ are things we here on earth simply cannot fathom:

"Eye has not seen, and ear has not heard, [nor has it] entered the human heart, what God has prepared for those who love Him" (1 Cor. 2:9).

But there's another factor to consider when dealing with this argument, a side issue (really just a variation on a theme) which many Protestants imagine has invincible biblical support. Protestant apologist Eric Svendsen, argues the point this way:

"The Scriptures insist that God *alone* enjoys this privilege[62] [of being able to know the private thoughts of someone] . . . 'Deal with each man according to all he does, since you know his heart (for you alone know the hearts of men) [1 Kings 8:39; 2 Chron. 6:30] . . . I the Lord search the heart and examine the mind (Jer. 17:10). . . and he who searches our hearts knows the mind of the Spirit (Rom. 8:27) . . . then all the churches will know that I am He who searches the hearts and minds'" (Rev. 2:23).[63]

---

[62] God does not "enjoy privileges." All of His divine attributes are proper to Him by nature and are not "privileges."

[63] Svendsen, *Protestant Answers*, 93.

Svendsen is confusing two categories: kind and degree. There are many of His divine attributes that God in His generosity communicates to His creatures. For example, God knows all things perfectly, though He has communicated to me, as part of my human nature, His attribute of knowing. I can know many things, but not perfectly, nor infinitely, as God does. The same is true of other attributes, such as loving, reasoning, and speaking. While it's absolutely true that in the category of *degree*, there is no comparison between how imperfectly I can do these things and how perfectly God can, but in the category of *kind*, it's clear that I can do these things (however imperfectly), just as God does. And all of this, of course, by the gift of God's grace. After all, men and women are created in God's image.[64]

This is why the passages Svendsen quotes here in no way conflicts with the Catholic teaching that we can invoke the intercession of the saints. In order to ask for their prayers, we must *ask* for their prayers! In other words, we communicate our request to the saints. Svendsen's argument crumbles here because he would have to admit that if he were to ask his pastor to pray for him, his pastor would *know his private thoughts* (ie. wanting prayer). Is that unbiblical? Of course not. The very nature of human discourse involves the communication of private thoughts by one person to another. And, as we saw a moment ago, God *intended* this by His communicating this attribute of His to us.[65]

---

[64] Cf. Gen. 1:26-27; CCC 355, 347, 380.
[65] Our ability as human beings to share in God's attributes

Svendsen is simply knocking down a straw man when he proclaims:

> "All of these passages assert or imply that God alone knows the private thoughts of a person. Neither Mary nor any other saint, no matter how exalted, can be considered anything more than a creature with all the attendant limitations."[66]

Catholics would respond to this irrelevant statement with a hearty, "Amen," and an equally hearty, "So what?"

Of *course* Mary and the saints are mere creatures, honored and cherished by God in heaven, but still creatures. Nobody argues that they aren't.[67] And yes, of course they are subject to all the limitations of human nature. But what Svendsen fails to recognize is that it simply isn't reasonable to ascribe to the blessed in heaven the same limitations under which we here on earth labor.

The other problem with Svendsen's argument is this: The Catholic Church does not teach that the saints are able to "look into our minds" unbidden and see what we're thinking. Svendsen falls again into the fallacy of the straw man by arguing against this fictional "Catholic position."[68]

Ultimately, Svendsen must still contend with the clear biblical evidence that God does in fact permit

---

is one more manifestation of God's supreme goodness. St. Bonaventure wrote that God shares His gifts with us "not to increase His glory, but to show it forth and to communicate it" (*In 2 Sent.* 1:2:2:1).

[66] Ibid. 93.

[67] Cf. CCC 301-323.

[68] As does Boettner, cf. *Roman Catholicism*, 150.

the saints in heaven to be aware of the acts and thoughts of people on earth. Scripture tells us that the blessed in heaven and the angels are aware of and rejoice over the repentance of even *one* sinner:

"I tell you, in just the same way there will be more joy in heaven over *one* sinner who repents than over ninety-nine righteous people who have no need of repentance. . . I tell you, there will be rejoicing among the angels of God over *one* sinner who repents" (Luke 15:7, 10).

Of course, we have no details about how they can know about individual repentances, but it would be absurd to argue, as Svendsen does, that simply because we don't understand *how* the blessed in heaven are able to do it that therefore they are unable to do it. We should never forget the Lord's promise of glorious and amazing abilities for His friends in heaven. St. Paul reminds us:

"So also is the resurrection of the dead. [The body] is sown corruptible; it is raised incorruptible. It is sown dishonorable; it is raised glorious. It is sown weak; it is raised powerful" (1 Cor. 15:42-43).

Perhaps the best and simplest way to summarize this point is to say that heaven is an amazing place filled with people who, by God's infinite grace, are capable of doing amazing things.

The Necromancy Argument

Some raise the necromancy[69] objection: "The saints

---

[69] "Necromancy" comes from the Greek compound of *nekros* (death) and *manteia* (divination).

are dead," they'll argue, "and the Bible forbids contact with the dead. Therefore, the Catholic practice of invoking the intercession of the saints is contrary to Scripture." This objection is rooted in a misunderstanding of the term necromancy.

Necromancy is an attempt to harness diabolical powers in order to, among other things, communicate with "familiar spirits." The Bible condemns this occultic practice, which includes attempting to communicate with spirits through trances, seances, and incantations.[70]

Necromancy is gravely sinful and has been condemned by the Catholic Church since the time of the early Fathers[71] down to our own age.[72]

But this has nothing to do with our asking saints to pray for us. Catholics should not be bothered by the necromancy argument. They should take the opportunity to explain that, aside from the method of communication, asking our fellow Christians in heaven to intercede on our behalf is no different from asking a fellow Christian here on earth to pray for us. We invoke their intercessions through mental prayer (this is to be strictly distinguished from the prayer of worship that's given to God alone). When a Christian asks the Blessed Virgin Mary or any other saint for prayer, he is not attempting to "conjure up" the spirit of that person. There is no effort

---

[70] Cf. Lev. 19:26, 31, 20:6, 27; Deut. 18:10-12; 1 Sam. 28:3-18; Is. 8:19, 19:3, 47:12-14.

[71] Cf. Tertullian, *Apologia* 23; *De Anima* 56-57; Lactantius, *Divinae Institutiones* 4:27.

[72] Cf. CCC 1852, 2110-2117.

made (there's not even the slightest thought!) to do anything other than ask for that person's intercession.

And besides, the saints aren't really dead at all. They're far more alive than we are on earth. Necromancy has to do with Satan, death, and the underworld. The saints are in heaven, face-to-face with God. Don't forget what Jesus said:

"Have you not read in the book of Moses, in the passage about the bush, how God told him, 'I am the God of Abraham, the God of Isaac, and the God of Jacob'? He is not the God of the dead but of the *living*. You are greatly misled" (Mark 12:26-27). [73]

When the Lord spoke these words to Moses on Mount Horeb, the three Patriarchs had been "dead" for many centuries.

A good question to ask a Protestant who claims that Christ absolutely forbids *any* contact between saints on earth and saints in heaven is: Why, in Matthew 17:1-8, did the Lord make a special point of appearing to Peter, James, and John on the Mount of Transfiguration in the company of Moses and Elijah — two "dead" saints?

---

[73] Cf. Wisdom 3:1-3; John 17:3.

Five

Praying for the Souls in Purgatory

THE BIBLE SAYS "our God is a consuming fire." Think of all the times in Scripture where God is depicted as fire: the burning bush in Exodus 3:1-6; the pillar of fire in Exodus 13:21-22, 14:24, and Numbers 14:14; the cloud of fire atop Mt. Sinai in Exodus 19:18 and 24:17; the tongues of fire on the day of Pentecost in Acts 2:3.[74]

> "The Lord Jesus is revealed from heaven with His mighty angels in flaming fire" (2 Thess. 1:7).

The fire of God's love is His instrument to purify us of our own selfishness, our inordinate attachment to creatures, and all the temporal punishments due to sin. This process of purification, Catholics call "purgatory." It is a passive process, meaning that the

---

[74] Cf. Psalm 50:3.

soul in purgatory does not *do* anything. The cleansing that takes place there is being done to him by the Lord.

The soul is not in purgatory for a "second chance." Purgatory is not a place where the soul works or earns or in any way does something to cleanse himself — all of this is done by God. Purgatory is not a place where people end up who are "too good" to go to hell and "not good enough" to go to heaven. These are all typical Protestant misunderstandings of this doctrine.

Purgatory actually has nothing whatsoever to do with salvation. Rather, it is a temporary phase of purification that only the saved can go through. The *Catechism* explains that,

> "All who die in God's grace and friendship,[75] but still imperfectly purified, are indeed assured of their eternal salvation; but after death they undergo purification, so as to achieve the holiness necessary to enter the joy of heaven" (CCC 1030).[76]

At the moment of our death, each of us will most likely have at least some vestiges of sin clinging to our souls. Any Protestant will admit that he is not

---

[75] Cf. Rom. 2:6-7, 11:22.

[76] The early Church was emphatic in its belief in purgatory and that the prayers of the living could assist the dead in Christ. Eg. Tertullian, *On The Soul* 58:1-2 (A.D. 208); St. Basil the Great, *Homilies on the Psalms* 7:2, 6 (A.D. 375); St. Gregory of Nyssa, *Sermon on the Dead* (A.D. 382); St. John Chrysostom, *Homilies on the Epistle to the Philippians* 3:4-10 (398); Serapion, *Prayer of the Eucharistic Sacrifice* 13:1-27 (A.D. 350).

spiritually perfect, even though he claims to have been "washed in the blood of Christ." This means that those imperfections and any selfishness must be eliminated before entering into heaven. Why?

> "But nothing unclean shall enter it, nor any one who practices abomination or falsehood, but only those who are written in the Lamb's book of life" (Rev. 21:27).

How is this process of purification carried out? In purgatory. Protestants will quickly condemn this Catholic doctrine as being "unbiblical," since (they think) it does not appear in Scripture. They condemn purgatory as being an insult to Christ, a way of saying that His redemptive suffering and death on the cross is insufficient to take care of us.[77] Nothing could be further from the truth.

As we just mentioned, purgatory has nothing to do with salvation. It has to do with cleansing the saved and preparing them for the eternal joys of heaven. Purgatory deals with the temporal effects due to sin; it does not deal with the eternal penalties merited by sin. Only Christ, through His death on the Cross, is capable of eradicating the eternal penalty due to sin. However, there are numerous effects of our sins that remain.

Christ's death on the cross did not eliminate the effects of sin in the temporal order. For example, two central consequences of the Original Sin[78] (ie. the "temporal punishments due to sin") are sickness

---

[77] Cf. James G. McCarthy, *The Gospel According to Rome* (Eugene: Harvest House, 1995), 110-117.

[78] Cf. Gen. 2:15-17, 3:1-19.

and death. Now, when Christ died on the cross, He redeemed us from the eternal penalty due to that sin (as well as all of our personal, actual sins), but He did not thereby eliminate the *temporal* effects that were caused by that sin: primarily sickness and death. The temporal effects due to sin extend, sadly, far beyond just physical illness and death.[79] They include the spiritual impurities and weaknesses that cling to the soul.

The Catholic Church teaches what the Bible itself teaches: This "final purification"[80] performed by God involves suffering. Let's look at St. Paul's teaching on the doctrine of purgatory:

> "According to the grace of God given to me, like a skilled master builder I laid a foundation, and another man is building upon it. Let each man take care how he builds upon it. For no other foundation can any one lay than that which is laid, which is Jesus Christ. Now if any one builds on the foundation with gold, silver, precious stones, wood, hay, straw — each man's work will become manifest; for the Day will disclose it, because it will be revealed with fire, and the fire will test what sort of work each one has done. If the work which any man has built on the foundation survives, he will receive a reward. If any man's work is burned up, he will suffer loss, though he himself will be saved, but only as through fire" (1 Cor. 3:10-15).

This passage, more than any other in Scripture, with the exception of 2 Maccabees 12, shows clearly

---

[79] In 1 Corinthians 11:27-32, St. Paul warns that certain sins can have lethal side effects.

[80] Cf. CCC 1031.

the essential elements of the doctrine of purgatory. Notice several key aspects of St. Paul's teaching here.

First, this process of disclosure takes place after death, at the moment the man stands before God and is judged for his life's contents — "It is appointed unto a man once to die, and then the judgment" (Heb. 9:27).

Second, this judgment involves a purification that purges away all the dross that clings to his soul, what St. Paul describes metaphorically as flammable materials such as "wood, hay, and straw." These materials are burned away in this judgment. Conversely, that man's good works — "gold, silver, and precious stones" — are refined and retained.

Third, this process of purification hurts; it involves suffering: "If any man's work is burned up, he will *suffer* loss." This means that the process described here is temporary in nature, since the man in question is destined for heaven: "He himself *will be* saved,[81] but only as passing through fire." This also indicates that this process of purification, "as though through fire," takes place before that man enters heaven.

All of this points to the fact that God, in His mercy, has prepared a way for those who die in the state of grace[82] and friendship with Him to have the imperfections and temporal punishments due to sin purged away by the fire of His love before they enter into heavenly glory.

---

[81] The future-tense Greek verb *sothésetai* is used here.
[82] Cf. Rom. 11:22.

Jesus also gave us a glimpse of a third state that exists after death — not heaven or hell:

"There was a rich man, who was clothed in purple and fine linen and who feasted sumptuously every day. And at his gate lay a poor man named Lazarus, full of sores, who desired to be fed with what fell from the rich man's table; moreover the dogs came and licked his sores. The poor man died and was carried by the angels to Abraham's bosom. The rich man also died and was buried; and in Hades, being in torment, he lifted up his eyes, and saw Abraham far off and Lazarus in his bosom. And he called out, 'Father Abraham, have mercy upon me, and send Lazarus to dip the end of his finger in water and cool my tongue; for I am in anguish in this flame.' But Abraham said, 'Son, remember that you in your lifetime received your good things, and Lazarus in like manner evil things; but now he is comforted here, and you are in anguish. And besides all this, between us and you a great chasm has been fixed, in order that those who would pass from here to you may not be able, and none may cross from there to us.' And he said, 'Then I beg you, father, to send him to my father's house, for I have five brothers, so that he may warn them, lest they also come into this place of torment.' But Abraham said, 'They have Moses and the prophets; let them hear them.' And he said, 'No, father Abraham; but if some one goes to them from the dead, they will repent.' He said to him, 'If they do not hear Moses and the prophets, neither will they be convinced if some one should rise from the dead'" (Luke 16:19-31).

Remember that Abraham and Lazarus were not in hell; nor were they in heaven — after all, Christ had not yet died on the cross, so the gates of heaven were still closed. They were in a special place of waiting (what theologians sometimes call the "Limbo of the Fathers"), where the souls of the just looked anxiously for Christ's redemptive sacrifice that would enable them to enter into heaven.[83] Furthermore, notice that in this passage, the Rich Man intercedes on behalf of his brothers still living on earth. Christ Himself gives us the evidence of a deceased person interceding on behalf of the living. Now, this would seem to indicate that the Rich Man, although in a place of "fiery torment," was not in hell. After all, the damned are incapable of showing charity, and the Rich Man was clearly doing so for his brothers.

In their attempt to refute purgatory, Protestants often misquote two passages, 2 Corinthians 5:6-8 and Philippians 1:21-23, which they think disprove the Catholic teaching.[84] Their argument goes like this: "The Bible says that 'to be absent from the body means to be present with the Lord.' So there is no biblical basis for thinking a Christian can go to any other location." But this is a simple misquoting of the texts. Look what they actually say:

> "So we are always of good courage; *we know that while we are at home in the body we are away from the Lord*, for we walk by faith, not by sight. We are of good courage, and *we would rather be away*

[83] Cf. Heb. 11:13-16, 32-40; 1 Pet. 3:18-22, 4:6.
[84] Examples of this deliberate and apparently deceitful verse-quoting sleight-of-hand are found in Loraine Boettner, *Roman Catholicism*, 226; James G. McCarthy, *The Gospel According to Rome*, 120.

from the body and at home with the Lord. So whether we are at home or away, we make it our aim to please Him. For we must all appear before the judgment seat of Christ, so that each one may receive good or evil, according to what he has done in the body" (2 Cor. 5:6-8).

"For to me to live is Christ, and to die is gain. If it is to be life in the flesh, that means fruitful labor for me. Yet which I shall choose I cannot tell. I am hard pressed between the two. My desire is to depart and be with Christ, for that is far better" (Phil. 1:21-23).

The doctrine of purgatory bears directly on the doctrine of the communion of saints. We pray for the repose of the souls of the dead that the Lord might shorten the time of their temporary suffering. In the same way that we would offer prayer on behalf of a fellow Christian here on earth that the Lord would lessen or eliminate the suffering caused by a physical illness, so too, we intercede for those in purgatory.[85]

Writing around the year 392, St. John Chrysostom pointed out the need for assisting the souls of the departed with our prayers:

"Let us help and commemorate them. If Job's sons were purified by their father's sacrifice,[86] why would we doubt that our offerings for the dead

---

[85] Scott Hahn, a convert from Evangelicalism, explains the biblical doctrine of purgatory in his five-tape audio set, "Answering Common Objections," available from St. Joseph Communications, P.O. Box 720, West Covina, CA 91793, (818) 526-2151.

[86] Cf. Job 1:5.

bring them some consolation? Let us not hesitate to help those who have died and to offer our prayers for them."[87]

St. Augustine wrote often on the subject of purgatory and prayers for the dead. Besides showing his own and the early Church's recognition that 2 Maccabees is part of the Old Testament canon of inspired Scripture (over against the Protestant argument that it is not), he summarized the early Church's teaching on purgatory and prayers for the dead in Christ:

> "We read in the book of Maccabees that the sacrifice was offered for the dead.[88] But even if it were found nowhere in the Old Testament writings, the authority of the universal Church which is clear on this point is of no small weight, where in the prayers of the priest poured forth to the Lord God at His altar the commendation of the dead has its place" (*The Care That Should Be Taken for the Dead* 1:3; cf. 15:18).

---

[87] *Homilies on First Corinthians* 41:5; cf. Tertullian, *The Crown* 3:4 (A.D. 211); *On Monogamy* 10:1-4 (A.D. 213).
[88] 2 Macc. 12:39-43.

Six

The Testimony of the Early Church

IN THE FIRST several centuries of the Church, we can see a rapid development of the doctrine of the communion of saints. Around the year A.D. 80, St. Clement, the Bishop of Rome, wrote his famous *Epistle to the Corinthians*.[89] The focus of Clement's letter was to help the Corinthian church resolve several problems that had arisen there. Besides the fact that this document is a clear example of the primacy of the bishop of Rome, it's revealing in other ways. For example, we get a glimpse into the Christian

---

[89] While the customary dating of this epistle is A.D. 96, convincing evidence has been brought forward by a number of patristics scholars in support of the view that it was actually written in 80. A concise discussion of the reasons in favor of the earlier date is found in William A. Jurgens, *The Faith of the Early Fathers* (Collegeville: The Liturgical Press, 1970), 1:6-7.

Church immediately after the apostolic period
(though while St. John was still alive). St. Clement
fills his Epistle with references to the Apostles,
Christian martyrs, and Old Testament heroes (cf.
Heb. 12:1-2). He exhorts the Corinthians to keep
ever in their minds the examples of the saints of the
Old and New Testaments:

> "Let us fix our eyes on those who perfectly served
> His magnificent glory. Let us take Enoch, for ex-
> ample, who was found righteous in obedience and
> so was taken up and did not experience death . . .
> "[90]

This emphasis on the virtues of the saints and
the reverent invocation of the Blessed Virgin Mary
and the saints, especially the martyrs, permeates the
life of the early Church. It bears directly on the Church's teaching on the nature of the communion of
saints, because it shows forth the early Christian
certitude that all Christians — those on earth, in purgatory, and in heaven — shared a genuine bond of
unity in and through Christ. This awareness of that
unity in Christ manifested itself throughout the writings of the Fathers, as well as in the hymns, art, and
sacred liturgies of the early Church.

The early Church's keen awareness of the communion of saints was rooted in its veneration of its
many martyrs, victims of Roman persecution in the
first few centuries after Christ. The early Christians'
love for their slain brethren was manifested in the
liturgies, hymns, prayers, and writings of the Fathers

---

[90] *Epistle to the Corinthians*, 9; cf. 19.

and Doctors. Masses were celebrated in honor of the martyrs. Mosaics depicting their lives and martyrdoms adorned countless ancient churchs.[91] Their intercession was universally invoked by the early Church. Their relics were safeguarded and venerated, and the moving accounts of their heroic deaths for Christ were carefully preserved, copied, and disseminated among the churches everywhere. The Catholic Church's theology of the communion of saints developed rapidly, and patristic writings that explain and emphasize the Church's honoring of the saints and reliance upon their heavenly intercession abound.

The late Church historian Henri Daniel-Rops describes this aspect of the early Church:

"The martyrs tended in every respect to disrupt Roman authority, simply by their patient suffering and their serene acceptance of self-sacrifice. . . . On the other hand, it need hardly be said that for their brethren in Christ their oblation had an explempary value whose importance cannot be over-estimated. Heroism has an appeal which is well known to anyone who has fought in a war and led men into battle. From the very first moment that the Roman state had begun to attack the Christians, it had put this powerful weapon of propaganda into their hands. The more public and widespread it made its persecutions, the more it worked to further that spread of the faith, through

---

[91] For a fascinating analysis of the prominence of veneration of the saints and martyrs in early Christian art and architecture (including over 100 photographs and drawings), see Yoram Tsafrir, ed., *Ancient Churches Revealed* (Jerusalem: Israel Exploration Society, 1993).

the blood of the martyrs, of which Tertullian had spoken."[92]

This chapter will examine briefly several representative selections from major early Church Fathers to show their teachings on aspects of the communion of saints. Though there is not enough space here to provide a detailed and systematic presentation of the early Church's entire teaching on this subject, these excerpts reflect its major elements.[93]

St. Cyril of Jerusalem (A.D. 315 - 386)

Among the early Church Fathers, one of the most luminous writers about the communion of saints was St. Cyril of Jerusalem.

As a young priest in Jerusalem, in the year 348, Cyril was commissioned by his bishop to compose a series of doctrinal sermons for the instruction and edification of the catechumens. These powerful, doctrinally-rich sermons are known as the *Catechetical Lectures*. In them, we find a treasure trove of evidence demonstrating that the Catholic Church's doctrines — not those of Evangelical Protestantism — were the ones held and taught by the early Church.

One of the most striking features of the *Catechetical Lectures* is that they're filled with Cyril's forceful teachings on such doctrines as the infallible

---

[92] Henri Daniel-Rops, *The Church of Apostles and Martyrs* (London: J.M. Dent & Sons, Ltd., 1960), 401.

[93] Cf. ibid., 515-517.

teaching office of the Catholic Church (18:23), the Mass as a sacrifice (23:6-8), the reality of purgatory and the efficacy of expiatory prayers for the dead (23:10), the Real Presence of Christ in the Eucharist (19:7; 21:3; 22:1-9), the theology of sacraments (1:3), the intercession of the saints (23:9), the sacrament of holy orders (23:2), the importance of frequent Communion (23:23), and baptismal regeneration (1:1-3; 3:10-12; 21:3-4). [94]

Here are several key excerpts from *Catechetical Lectures*, where St. Cyril discusses the Church's teaching on the communion of saints, specifically how Christians should invoke the intercession of the saints during the sacrifice of the Mass:

> "Having sanctified ourselves by these spiritual hymns, we beseech the merciful God to send forth His Holy Spirit upon the gifts lying before him [ie. the bread and wine], that he may make the bread the Body of Christ and the wine the Blood of Christ; for whatsoever the Holy Ghost has touched, is surely sanctified and changed. Then, after the spiritual sacrifice,[95] the bloodless service

---

[94] One key reason to acquaint Evangelicals with the writings of Cyril of Jerusalem (as well as those of the other Fathers) is that the doctrines he teaches so forcefully are the very same Catholic doctrines that Evangelicals claim are not found in Scripture and were "invented" by the Catholic Church at a much later date.

[95] Notice the heavy emphasis St. Cyril places on the *sacrificial* character of the ancient Mass. This identification of the Eucharist as a sacrifice is common among the early Fathers. The early Christian Eucharistic celebration, which he describes in such elaborate detail, bears no resemblance whatsoever to the "Sunday service" of today's Evangelical and Fundamentalist churches. For a

is completed, over the sacrifice of propitiation we entreat God for the common peace of the Churches, for the welfare of the world, for kings, for soldiers and allies, for the sick, for the afflicted and, in a word, for all who stand in need of succor we all pray and offer this sacrifice.

"Then we commemorate also those who have fallen asleep before us, first the patriarchs, prophets, apostles, and martyrs, that at their prayers and intercessions God would receive our petition. Then on behalf also of the holy Fathers and bishops who have fallen asleep before us and, in a word, of all who in past years have fallen asleep among us, believing that it will be a very great benefit to the souls for whom the supplication is put up [ie. offered up to God] while that holy and most awful sacrifice is set forth.

"I wish to persuade you by an illustration. For I know that many say, 'what is a soul profited, which departs from this world either with sins or without sins, if it be commemorated in the prayer?' Well, if a king were to banish certain [people] who had given him offense, and then

detailed historical analysis of the sacrifice of the Mass in the early Church, I recommend: Adalbert Hamman, O.F.M., ed., *The Mass: Ancient Liturgies and Patristic Texts* (Staten Island: Alba House, 1967); Joseph A. Jungman, S.J., *The Mass of the Roman Rite: Its Origins and Development* (Dublin: Four Courts Press, 1955) 2 volumes; James L. Meagher, *How Christ Said the First Mass* (Rockford: TAN Books and Publishers, 1984 ed.); Jerome Gassner, O.S.B., *The Canon of the Mass: Its History, Theology, and Art* (St. Louis: Herder, 1950); and the massive historical analysis by Casimir Kucharek, *The Byzantine-Slav Liturgy of St. John Chrysostom* (Combermere, ONT: Alleluia Press: 1971).

those who belong to them should weave a crown and offer it to him on behalf of those under punishment, would he not grant a remission of their penalties? In the same way, we, when we offer to him our supplications for those who have fallen asleep, though they be sinners, weave no crown but [rather] offer up Christ sacrificed for our sins, propitiating our merciful God for them as well as for ourselves."[96]

St. Jerome (A.D. 347-419)

St. Jerome was born in the town of Stridon in what is now known as the region of Croatia and Dalmatia. He had a stunning command of biblical languages, and is recognized not just for his profound theological acumen, but also for being one of the greatest biblical scholars the Church has ever produced. He was also known for his sarcastic wit, a pronounced attitude of pride, and his querulous temperament. Nonetheless, his ascetical life and deep prayer life helped soften his rough edges and he became a great and holy saint.

This priest-scholar was for a time the personal secretary and translator for Pope Damasus I (382-385), after which he went to live permanently as a monk in Bethlehem, where he studied Hebrew.

St. Jerome gives us insight into his own attitude toward the authority of the bishop of Rome in this passage from his letter to Pope Damasus I:

[96] *Catechetical Lectures* 23:7-10; English translation: Philip Schaff, Henry Wace, editors, *Nicene and Post-Nicene Fathers* (Peabody, MA: Hendrickson Publishers, 1995 ed.), 7:154-155.

> "I follow no leader but Christ and I join in communion with none but your Blessedness, that is, with the Chair of Peter. I know that this is the rock on which the Church has been built. Whoever eats the Lamb [ie. the Holy Eucharist] outside this house is profane" (*Epistle 15* [A.D. 374]).

Like any faithful Catholic, St. Jerome aligned his theology not with a *sola scriptura* approach to doctrine (I'll decide for myself what *I* think the Bible means); rather, he submitted his brilliant mind to the mind of the Church. Notice how, in this letter *Against Vigilantius* (a heretic), he describes the early Church's teaching:

> "You say in your book that while we live we are able to pray for each other, but afterwards when we have died, the prayer of no person for another can be heard; and this is especially clear since the martyrs, though they cry for vengeance for their own blood, have never been able to obtain their request. But if the Apostles and martyrs while still alive in the body can pray for others, at a time when they ought still to be solicitous about themselves, how much more will they do so after their crowns, victories, and triumphs!" (*Against Vigilantius* 6 [A.D. 406]).

St. John Chrysostom (A.D. 347-407)

St. John Chrysostom was famous for his eloquence in expounding Catholic doctrine. So marvelous a speaker was he that his contemporaries took to calling him Chrysostom, which is Greek for "golden mouth."

In this citation, we see him mention that prayers and intercessions of those he calls the "holy fathers" (ie. departed Christians — now saints in heaven) have a helpful effect on Christians who have not yet died and who benefit from these prayers.

> "God forbid that any in this fair assembly should appear there suffering such things! But by the prayers of the holy fathers, correcting all our offenses and having shown forth the abundant fruit of virtue, may we depart hence [ie. to heaven] with much confidence through the grace and loving kindness of our Lord Jesus Christ . . . " (*Homily* 6:19).

St. Augustine of Hippo (A.D. 354-430)

St. Augustine, more than any of the other early Fathers, is looked to with reverence by many Protestants, especially by the Reformed churches. It's crucial, therefore, that they be aware of his teachings on the subject of the communion of saints. Among the Fathers, especially the Latin Fathers, St. Augustine is regarded as embodying the pinnacle of theological and biblical insight in the Western Church. We'll look at a series of his statements, written between 380 and 430, covering aspects of his teachings on this doctrine.

> "There is an ecclesiastical discipline, as the faithful know, when the names of the martyrs are read aloud in that place at the altar of God [ie. at Mass], where the prayer is not offered for them. Prayer, however, is offered for other dead who are remembered. For it is wrong to pray for a martyr,

to whose prayers we ought ourselves to be commended" (*Sermon 159*).

In this next passage from the writings of St. Augustine, notice how he links the Christian doctrine of praying for the repose of the souls of the faithful departed with the sacrifice of the Mass. He shows that our prayers are efficacious for them, just as the prayers of Mary and the saints in heaven are efficacious for us:

"By the prayers of the Holy Church, and by the salvific sacrifice [of the Mass], and by the alms which are given for their spirits, there is no doubt that the dead are aided, that the Lord might deal with them more mercifully than their sins would deserve. For the whole Church observes this practice which was handed down by the Fathers, that it prays for those who have died in the communion of the Body and the Blood of Christ, when they are commemorated in their own place in the sacrifice itself, and the sacrifice is offered also in memory of them, on their behalf. If, then, works of mercy are celebrated for the sake of those who are being remembered, who would hesitate to recommend them, on whose behalf prayers to God are not offered in vain? It is not at all to be doubted that such prayers are of profit to the dead" (*Sermon 172*).

"The prayer either of the Church herself, or of certain pious individuals is heard on behalf of certain of the dead" (*The City of God* 21:24:2).[97]

---

[97] Other examples of St. Augustine's teaching on the communion of saints are found in *Against Faustus the Manichean* 19:13:1-5, 20:21:4-6; *The City of God* 20:9:2; and *The Care That Should Be Taken for the Dead*.

As for St. Augustine's attitude toward Mary and her role in the Church, patristic historian Frederic van der Meer says:

"[St. Augustine] recognizes what had been by then become the classical antithesis between Mary and Eve as a great sacrament. He knows of Mary's privileges and of her virginity before, during, and after the birth of Christ;[98] he knows of her sinlessness. Though he recognizes the righteousness of Joseph, yet he counts both Joseph and all the other righteous men of the past among the sinners, but where Mary is concerned he will 'for the honor of the Lord, not hear of such a thing as sin.'"[99]

St. John Damascene (A.D. 657-749)

This great Father from the Eastern Church was born in Damascus, Syria, at a time of great turmoil in the Church.[100] Not only had Islam overrun the formerly Christian Mediterranean world, there were also serious doctrinal wranglings taking place within the Church.

One of the most vexing was the controversy over the use of statues and icons venerating our Lord, the Virgin Mary, and the saints. Those who

---

[98] Cf. *Epistles* 137:5:8; 162:6; 186:1; 188:4; 191:2; 215:3.
[99] *De Natura et Gratia, ad Timasium et Jacobum, contra Pelagium*, I, 36, 42.
[100] The iconoclastic heresy and St. John Damascene's refutation of it is explained in Phillip Hughes, *A History of the Church* (London: Sheed & Ward, Ltd., 1948) 2:118-126; cf. Warren H. Carroll, *The Building of Christendom* (Front Royal: Christendom Press, 1987), 2:276-366.

opposed this practice were called the iconoclasts. Those who upheld it were considered orthodox by St. John Damascene, who wrote and preached widely on this issue. He entered the monastery of St. Sabas in Palestine, near Jerusalem, where he composed his brilliant works on dogmatic and moral theology. He was ordained a priest and spent his days in prayer, writing, and preaching. Scholars regard his most important work to be *De Fide Orthodoxa* (Latin: On the Orthodox Faith), and it is here that we find some of his most luminous statements concerning how the early Christians and the Christians of his own day honored Mary and the saints, and venerated the relics of the saints, especially of martyrs.

> "Assuredly, she [Mary] who played the part of the Creator's servant and mother is in all strictness and truth in reality God's mother and Lady and queen over all created things. . . To the saints honor must be paid as friends of Christ, as sons and heirs of God. In the words of John the theologian and Evangelist, 'As many as received Him, to them He gave power to become sons of God. So that they are no longer servants but sons, and if sons then also heirs, heirs of God and joint heirs with Christ.' And the Lord in the holy Gospels says to His apostles, 'You are my friends. Henceforth I call you not servants, for the servant does not know what his Lord does' (John 15:15). . . Surely, then, the worshippers and friends and sons of God are to be held in honor. For the honor shown to the most thoughtful of fellow-servants is a proof of good feeling towards the common master."[101]

---

[101] Cf. Basil of Caesarea, *Panegyric Homily* 19, *In Sanctos*

Seven

The Veneration of Relics

"PRECIOUS IN THE SIGHT of the Lord is the death of His saints" (Ps. 116:15). This brief passage is a wonderfully concise explanation of the reason why Catholics venerate martyrs and their relics.

Notice that Scripture says that the very *death* of the saints is precious to the Lord. The Catholic Church recognizes that there is an intrinsic worth and a beauty in the death of a holy Christian. The Church's immense esteem for these holy men and women was evident from the very beginning.[102]

"St. Cyprian, in a letter to some Christians who were awaiting martyrdom, begged them not to

---

Quadraginta Martyres.

[102] St. Augustine spoke at length of the early Church's reverence for the relics of the saints and martyrs in *The Care That Should Be Taken for the Dead* 5-20.

forget him when they were in glory. What the Christian heroes proclaimed, therefore, was the certainty of a victory surpassing all earthly triumphs; and the cult of their memory, of their relics and of their tombs, which was to undergo a tremendous development during the third century before it bloomed in all its glory on the morrow of [the Emperor] Constantine's Peace, linked together in a communion of saints the Church militant on earth and the Church in heaven whose triumph carried the pledge of final victory. *'Tu vincis inter martyres!'* declares an Ambrosian hymn which the Catholic Church still sings on the feasts of martyrs. Through the sufferings of His saints Christ's triumph was ensured."[103]

So now we come to the important though subsidiary issue of whether or not it is proper to honor the bodily remains of the saints, as well as objects that came into contact with them during their earthly life.

At this point in our examination of the general subject of the communion of saints, given the biblical and historical evidence we've just looked at, the Protestant might grudgingly admit that Catholics are not wrong for *honoring* martyrs, but he's still uneasy about the idea of *venerating* their relics — fragments of their bones!

To overcome this objection, as with the other issues we've examined, we need to consider what the Bible says about such things. Perhaps the best place to start is the Old Testament episode of Elisha's bones.

---

[103] Daniel-Rops, *The Church of Apostles and Martyrs*, 402.

"So Elisha died, and they buried him. Now bands of Moabites used to invade the land in the spring of the year. And as a man was being buried, lo, a marauding band was seen and the man was cast into the grave of Elisha; and as soon as the man touched the bones of Elisha, he revived, and stood on his feet" (2 Kings 13:20-21).

This is a striking example of the power of grace God invests in the relics of His saints. True, not all relics of saints have miraculous characteristics, but the Bible is definitely clear that some do. In this particular biblical account involving the remains of Elisha, Scripture shows us that there is nothing strange or "unbiblical" about the Catholic claim that God works miracles through the remains of His saints. As with so many other contested points of Catholic doctrine, it's enough to simply show that a given Catholic belief, such as miracles being worked through relics, or Mary's Bodily Assumption, is compatible with Scripture, if not actually formally taught.

But in the case of relics, we have ample biblical evidence to demonstrate two key points pertaining to the Catholic Church's teaching on relics: First, the Bible is clear that, from time to time, God wishes to perform miracles through the relics of His saints. Second, we see that it is not only permissible to venerate these relics, it is proper and praiseworthy to do so.

Consider these other passages:

"As He went, the people pressed round Him. And a woman who had had a flow of blood for twelve years and could not be healed by any one, came up behind Him, and touched the fringe of His garment; and immediately her flow of blood ceased. And Jesus said, 'Who was it that touched me?' When all denied it, Peter said, 'Master, the multitudes surround you and press upon you!' But Jesus said, 'Someone touched me; for I perceive that power has gone forth from me.' And when the woman saw that she was not hidden, she came trembling, and falling down before Him declared in the presence of all the people why she had touched Him, and how she had been immediately healed. And He said to her, 'Daughter, your faith has made you well; go in peace'" (Luke 8:42-48).

"And when the men of that place recognized Him, they sent round to all that region and brought to Him all that were sick, and besought Him that they might only touch the fringe of His garment; and as many as touched it were made well" (Matt. 14:35-36).

"And wherever He came, in villages, cities, or country, they laid the sick in the market places, and besought Him that they might touch even the fringe of His garment; and as many as touched it were made well" (Mark 6:56).

"And God did extraordinary miracles by the hands of Paul, so that handkerchiefs or aprons were carried away from his body to the sick, and diseases left them and the evil spirits came out of them" (Acts 19:11-12).

"[T]hey even carried out the sick into the streets, and laid them on beds and pallets, that as Peter came by at least his shadow might fall on some of them. The people also gathered from the towns around Jerusalem, bringing the sick and those afflicted with unclean spirits, and they were all healed" (Acts 5:14-16).

Because the bodies of the saints (as with all Christians) were the living temples of the Holy Spirit[104] and, on the Last Day, will be awakened by Christ and glorified, it's proper to honor them. And the biblical evidence is clear that God sometimes bestows miracles and graces through them.

---

[104] Cf. 1 Cor. 3:16, 6:19; 2 Cor. 6:16.

Eight

Statues and Images

SOONER OR LATER, Protestants get around to this issue. The Catholic practice of using statues, icons, crucifixes, and other sacred images to depict Christ, the Virgin Mary, and the saints, is offensive to them.

They object to this practice on the grounds that it violates the biblical injunction against images in Exodus 20:3-6.

> "And God spoke all these words, saying, 'I am the Lord your God, who brought you out of the land of Egypt, out of the house of bondage. You shall have no other gods before me. You shall not make for yourself a graven image, or any likeness of anything that is in heaven above, or that is in the earth beneath, or that is in the water under the earth; you shall not bow down to them or serve them; for I the Lord your God am a jealous God, visiting the iniquity of the fathers upon the

children to the third and the fourth generation of those who hate me, but showing steadfast love to thousands of those who love me and keep my commandments.'"[105]

Let's analyze this passage and see if it really supports the Protestant argument against the Catholic use of statues and icons.

First, notice that God is here forbidding the making of any type of image, graven or otherwise, for the purpose of idolatry. Worshipping anything other than the One True God is idolatry, and the Israelites were prone to fall into that sin.

The purpose of this commandment is to keep the Israelites (indeed, all of God's faithful people in whatever era) away from idolatry. Consider these stern warnings:

> "Cursed be the man who makes a graven or molten image, an abomination to the Lord, a thing made by the hands of a craftsman, and sets it up in secret. And all the people shall answer and say, 'Amen'" (Deut. 27:12).

> "For the wrath of God is revealed from heaven against all ungodliness and wickedness of men who by their wickedness suppress the truth. For what can be known about God is plain to them, because God has shown it to them. Ever since the creation of the world His invisible nature, namely, His eternal power and deity, has been clearly perceived in the things that have been made. So they

---

[105] The parallel passage is Deuteronomy 5:6-9. Examples of condemnation of idol worship are found in Num. 33:52; Deut. 7:5, 25, 9:12, 12:3; 2 Kings 17:9-18, 23:24; 2 Chron. 23:17, 28:1-3, 33:18-25, 34:1-7.

are without excuse; for although they knew God they did not honor Him as God or give thanks to Him, but they became futile in their thinking and their senseless minds were darkened. Claiming to be wise, they became fools, and *exchanged the glory of the immortal God for images resembling mortal man or birds or animals or reptiles"* (Rom. 1:18-23).

Clearly, God detests idolatry. But does this mean that His commandment in Exodus 20 absolutely prohibits the making of statues or images of any kind? No.

There are many legitimate purposes for using statues and images — ones with which Protestants don't quarrel. For example, having pictures of loved ones in your wallet or on the mantelpiece in your home is a legitimate use of images. In the case of deceased or absent friends or relatives, these pictures represent people that are not physically present. Nobody complains that having such pictures violates God's commandment against images. Why? Because common sense tells us that they don't.

Another example: Protestants accept the use of statues to depict dead national heroes, such as the Lincoln Memorial, statues of military figures, and other personalities. Obviously, such statues are made for the purpose of reminding us of deceased people, but nobody in his right mind would assume that people worship these statues.

But these more mundane examples will only make our case up to a point. So now let's up the ante and ask a more challenging question: Does the Lord's commandment in Exodus 20 prohibit the

making and use of statues for *religious* purposes?
No, it doesn't. Elsewhere in Scripture, God actually
commands that statues and other graven images be
carved for religious purposes.

> "[God said] make two cherubim of gold; of ham-
> mered work shall you make them, on the two
> ends of the mercy seat. Make one cherub on the
> one end, and one cherub on the other end. . . .
> You shall make the tabernacle with . . . cherubim
> skillfully worked" (Ex. 25:18-19, 26:1).

> "The Lord said to Moses, 'Make a fiery serpent,
> and set it on a pole; and every one who is bitten,
> when he sees it, shall live.' So Moses made a
> bronze serpent, and set it on a pole" (Num.
> 21:8-9).

In the following passages, we see Solomon di-
recting that various statues and carved images be
made and used to adorn the Temple.[106] Notice in
particular the first passage, where two large statues
of angels are placed in the Holy of Holies, to represent the sacredness of that liturgical space and the
presence of God's holy angels:

> "He made two cherubim of olivewood, each ten
> cubits high. . . He put the cherubim in the inner-
> most part of the Temple . . . And he overlaid the
> cherubim with gold. He carved all the walls of the
> Temple round about with carved figures of cheru-
> bim and palm trees and open flowers" (1 Kings
> 6:23, 27-29).

---

[106] Cf. 1 Kings 7:18, 29, 36, 42, 44. Another example of God
approving the use of images is found in the rather hu-
morous episode of 1 Samuel 6:1-18.

"[The brazen sea] stood upon [statues of] twelve oxen, three facing north, three facing west, three facing south, and three facing east" (1 Kings 7:25).

"And on the surfaces of its stays and on its panels, he carved cherubim, lions, and palm trees, according to the space of each, with wreaths round about" (1 Kings 7:36).

Perhaps the most striking thing about these examples of Solomon making and using statues and images for religious purposes is that it was done as a result of the gift of wisdom that God had granted him (cf. 1 Kings 31-28; 9-14). What's even more remarkable is what the Bible tells us occurred just as Solomon was beginning his construction of the Temple:

"Now the word of the Lord came to Solomon, 'Concerning this house which you are building, *if you will walk in my statutes and obey my ordinances and keep all my commandments and walk in them*, then I will establish my word with you, which I spoke to David your father. And I will dwell among the children of Israel, and will not forsake my people Israel'" (1 Kings 11-13).

What does Solomon do in light of this warning from God to "walk in His statutes and obey His ordinances and keep all His commandments"? He carves statues and images.

And in doing this (making and using statues for religious purposes) Solomon was clearly *not* violating God's command in Exodus 20 and Deuteronomy 5 regarding idolatry. Why? Because these carved statues and images were not intended for any idolatrous purpose. At that time in salvation history, nobody would have thought of worshipping them as idols. No, these images had a legitimate, sanctified purpose in God's eyes, and Scripture says He approved of them:

> "When Solomon had finished building the house of the Lord and the king's house and all that Solomon desired to build, the Lord appeared to Solomon a second time, as He had appeared to him at Gibeon. And the Lord said to him, 'I have heard your prayer and your supplication, which you have made before me; I have consecrated this house which you have built, and put my name there for ever; my eyes and my heart will be there for all time'" (1 Kings 9:1-3).

This evidence, perhaps more than any other biblical example, shows conclusively that God not only tolerates the proper use of statues and images for religious purposes, but He is *pleased* by it.

This is true, of course, of the Catholic use of statues and images of our Lord, the Blessed Virgin Mary, and the saints. These images are used to honor and better remember the Lord Jesus Christ, His Mother, and His friends, the angels and saints in heaven.

Nine

Does Honoring Mary and the Saints Offend God?

"ALTHOUGH CATHOLICS deny that they worship and adore Mary, they generally contradict that denial by their practice." This is how one Evangelical Protestant apologist begins his argument against the Catholic Church.[107] Let's see if his "Mary worship" charge has any merit.

Now that we've looked at the evidence supporting images of Mary and the saints, it's important to point out how the Church has dealt with the issue of "Mary worship" — both the baseless charges as well as actual occurrences.

---

[107] Eric Svendsen, *Protestant Answers: A Response to Recent Attacks Against Protestant Theology by Catholic Apologists* (Atlanta: New Testament Restoration Foundation Publications, 1995), 92.

"There seems to be some confusion on the part of Catholics as to what worship is. They insist in their writings that Mary is to receive honor, not worship; but their explicit practice more resembles worship than honor — bowing to, praying to, and singing praises to anyone must be considered worship, not mere honor."

If anyone is confused, it would appear to be Mr. Svendsen. His argument is quite muddled. First, let's recognize that in Scripture it's common to read of "singing praises" to God, something Catholics and Protestants would agree is an excellent and necessary thing to do. But what about the biblical examples of "singing praises" to humans?

For example, it's interesting that God would inspire the following words to be written in Scripture, including the prophecy that there would be "bowing to" and "praising" of Judah, a mere human being:[108]

"Judah, your brothers shall praise you; your hand shall be on the neck of your enemies; your father's sons shall bow down before you" (Gen. 49:7).

"The Lord has declared this day concerning you that you are a people for His own possession, as He has promised you, and that you are to keep all His commandments, that He will set you high above all nations that He has made, in praise and in fame and in honor, and that you shall be a people holy to the Lord your God, as He has spoken" (Deut. 26:18-19).

"Praise His people, O you nations; for He avenges the blood of His servants, and takes vengeance on

---

[108] Cf. Zeph. 3:19.

His adversaries, and makes expiation for the land of His people" (Deut. 32:43).

The Bible doesn't merely speak approvingly of men rendering such legitimate praise to other human beings. More importantly, it gives many examples of where God Himself praises faithful men and women. Here are some examples:

"He is a Jew who is one inwardly, and real circumcision is a matter of the heart, spiritual and not literal. His praise is not from men but from God" (Rom. 2:29).

How is it that God praises human beings and we are not permitted to do so? Where does the Bible offer even the slightest support for Svendsen's (and Protestantism's) view? It does not. This type of argumentation is clearly absurd. And don't forget that the Holy Spirit inspired St. Paul to write:

"Be imitators of me, as I am of Christ. *I praise you* because you remember me in everything and maintain the traditions even as I have delivered them to you" (1 Cor. 11:1-2).

As for bowing, Svendsen's "all or nothing" approach to Scripture, so typical of modern-day Evangelical anti-Catholic polemics, simply doesn't pan out. It's inconsistent with the Scriptural evidence. He'd have a hard time (if he's to be consistent with his own argument that "bowing to . . . anyone must be considered worship, not mere honor") explaining how the Patriarch Isaac could utter these prophetic words to his son Jacob:

"Let peoples serve you, and nations bow down to

you. Be lord over your brothers, and may your mother's sons bow down to you" (Gen. 27:29).

Joshua bowed down and did obeisance before an angel, but committed no sin in doing so (Joshua 5:14). Ruth bowed down to the ground before Boaz in gratitude (Ruth 2:8-10), but she was not *worshipping* Boaz. The Shunammite Woman bowed down before the Prophet Elisha after he had raised her child from the dead (2 Kings 4:37), but she was not committing idolatry by doing so. Neither was Lot, when he "bowed down" before two angels of the Lord in Genesis 19:1. Nor was David sinning against God's commandment when he "bowed down and did obeisance" before King Saul (1 Sam. 24:8). Bathsheba and Nathan the Prophet were also blameless when they "bowed down in honor" before King David, while the monarch was on his deathbed (1 Kings 1:16, 25).[109] When Jacob and Essau had their dramatic reconciliation, we read:

> "He himself went on before them, bowing himself to the ground seven times, until he came near to his brother" (Gen. 33:3).

And then there are the words of Christ concerning the honor and glory due to faithful Christians:

> "I know your works. Behold, I have set before you an open door, which no one is able to shut; I know that you have but little power, and yet you have kept my word and have not denied my name. Behold, I will make those of the synagogue

---

[109] Other examples of legitimate bowing down in honor before human beings are found in Gen. 23:7-13, 33:4-7, 42:5, 43:26-29, 48:9; Num. 22:31; 1 Sam. 20:41; 25:41.

of Satan who say that they are Jews and are not, but lie — behold, *I will make them come and bow down before your feet,* and learn that I have loved you" (Rev. 3:8-9).

If, as Svendsen and other Protestants argue, "praising" and "bowing down" before a human being "must be considered worship, not mere honor," then the Bible indicts St. Paul and the Lord Jesus Christ himself, since they are caught in the act of praising and honoring human beings! One can see how this type of crabbed argumentation, so common to Protestant polemics against the Catholic Church, is hollow. Svendsen's arguments here are good examples of the shallowness of the standard anti-Catholic arguments against the communion of saints.

The biblical evidence we've just examined shows us two things: a) The mere act of bowing, if it is an action performed to show respect and honor to a friend of God, is not just tolerable, but admirable; and b) Honoring and praising God's friends is a good thing and it is a way to honor and glorify God.

Why Should We Honor the Saints?

Scripture tells us that if we persevere in fidelity to Christ, we will receive honor and praise from Him and His friends. This is what the Catholic Church teaches and does when it honors and praises Mary and the saints.

"In this you rejoice, though now for a little while you may have to suffer various trials, so that the genuineness of your faith, more precious than gold which though perishable is tested by fire, may redound to *praise and glory and honor* at the revelation of Jesus Christ" (1 Peter 1:6-7).

When we recognize and proclaim the beauty God has wrought in a majestic mountain, or a dazzling sunset, no one would think that doing so somehow takes away any glory from God. God is glorified in His creation (eg. angels, mountains, stars, sunsets, human beings), and when we praise the beauty of His creation we are praising Him. This principle is at the heart of the Catholic teaching on honoring Mary and the saints. We recognize the great beauty and the graces God has bestowed on these men and women,[110] and praising them redounds to God's greater honor and glory.

On the other hand, bowing before anything or anyone in an act of worship is, of course, idolatry.[111] The Catholic Church has always made this distinction clear. The Bible makes this clear, too.[112] We should also remember, though, that the saints themselves are held out in Scripture as being worthy of praise and emulation. St. Paul said:

"Our gospel came to you not only in word, but also in power and in the Holy Spirit and with full conviction. You know what kind of men we

---

[110] Cf. Rom. 8:30.

[111] Cf. CCC 2112-2114.

[112] Cf. Judges 2:17, 16:30; Rom. 11:4. The Hebrew word for "bow down," *shachah,* means "to lie prostrate." The same word is used both in the passages that prohibit bowing (eg. Ex. 20:5) and in some of those that show bowing as legitimate (eg. Gen. 27:29).

nroved to be among you for your sake. *And you became imitators of us and of the Lord*, for you received the word in much affliction, with joy inspired by the Holy Spirit; so that *you became an example to all the believers* in Macedonia and in Achaia. For not only has the word of the Lord sounded forth from you in Macedonia and Achaia, *but your faith in God has gone forth everywhere*, so that we need not say anything" (1 Thess. 1:5-8).

Even Martin Luther, well after he had renounced the Catholic Church and had become a Protestant, spoke of Mary in these glowing terms:

"She, the lady above heaven and earth, must . . . have a heart so humble that she might have no shame in washing the swaddling clothes or preparing a bath for St. John the Baptist, like a servant girl. What humility! It would surely have been more just to have arranged for her a golden coach, pulled by 4,000 horses, and to cry and proclaim as the carriage proceeded, 'Here passes the woman who is raised above the whole human race!' . . . She was not filled with pride by this praise . . . this immense praise: 'No woman is like unto thee! *Thou art more than an empress or a queen* . . . blessed above all nobility, wisdom, or saintliness!'"[113]

---

[113] *Luther's Works* 21:327, 36:208, 45:107. Statements of praise for Mary like these are sources of scandal and irritation for today's Evangelical Protestants. But in reality, they serve to show just how far Evangelicalism has drifted from its own roots. Today's Protestant antagonism against Catholic teachings on Mary and the saints arises not from any authentic, organic doctrinal system, but from five centuries of accreted hostility towards things Catholic.

Imitating the Saints

In that last passage of Scripture, not only do we see St. Paul pleased that the Thessalonian Christians diligently imitated him and his apostolic companions, he also points out that they themselves had by then become objects of emulation for other Christians ("you became an example").

He speaks of their example as "going everywhere" and shows that it is good to recognize the holiness of God's saints (whether they're on earth or, by implication, in heaven) and imitate them. In so doing, as St. Paul reminds us, we become saintly too, and this leads to our example being an encouragement to others.

There are several other passages we should consider as we see what the Bible says about Christians on earth honoring and emulating the saints.

> "Brethren, join in imitating me, and mark those who so live as you have an example in us. . . Finally, brethren, whatever is true, whatever is honorable, whatever is just, whatever is pure, whatever is lovely, whatever is gracious, if there is any excellence, *if there is anything worthy of praise, think about these things.* What you have learned and received and heard and seen in me, do; and the God of peace will be with you" (Phil. 3:17, 4:8-9).

The Protestant who objects that this conclusion involves a misapplication of this passage will have to explain why the saints should be excluded from those things that are honorable, just, and worthy of praise.

Furthermore, there are several important components of these two passages from Philippians that we must consider. First, notice that we're told to think about honorable, pure, and just things. The Blessed Virgin Mary and the saints in heaven are the *epitome* of honorable, just, and worthy of praise — they have received from God the highest honor and praise possible, and they have been perfected in righteousness (cf. Heb. 12:23). So, biblically speaking, Christians are not just permitted to reflect on and speak about the saints, we are *exhorted* to do so.

Second, we see in Philippians 3:17 St. Paul's statement, "join in imitating me." Protestants generally feel uncomfortable with the Catholic emphasis on the saints, suspecting that such focusing on them somehow robs Christ of attention. But nothing could be further from the truth.

Here we see that St. Paul wants others to imitate him, just as he was striving to imitate Christ. It's not an "either or" approach here — either the saints or God — but a "both and" attitude. Imitate Christ *and* imitate those who were exemplary in imitating Him.

This, of course, is what the Catholic Church is doing when it encourages devotion to Mary and the saints. They are the models for us in Christian sanctity, heroism, and fidelity to Christ's gospel. When we focus our attentions on the saints, we are simply carrying out the excellent advice given to us by St. Paul.

Third, notice that St. Paul tells his readers they

(like we) should "do" (ie. practice and believe) the things they saw and learned from him. What were those things?

In the realm of imitating virtue, St. Paul showed himself to be zealous, diligent, brave, charitable, prayerful, kind, joyful, full of faith, a lover of Scripture and the Church, and above all, unswerving in his love for Christ.

These are precisely the things each of us is called to be, and St. Paul holds himself out as an example. Remember that he was not merely telling his first-century readers to meditate on his example and follow it. The Holy Spirit inspired those words and preserved them in the Church for us. This means that you and I are called to focus our thoughts on all the saints — God's friends — as models for us to follow.

> "Remember your leaders, those who spoke to you the word of God; consider the outcome of their life, and imitate their faith" (Heb. 13:7).

In the realm of "doing" the things St. Paul handed on,[114] we see the whole body of apostolic doctrine and practice that he received from the Lord and handed on to the Church. Part of the reason Catholics emphasize devotion to the saints is that we see in them a profound understanding of and fidelity to the doctrines of the Faith; doctrines handed down to them from Christ and the Apostles, and

---

[114] The term "handed on" is the English equivalent of the Greek verb used here, *paredoka*, from which we get the word "tradition." St. Jerome rendered *paredoka* into Latin as: *"tradidi"* (what I *traditioned* [to you]).

which they handed down to us in the writings, preaching, and by the way they lived out these teachings.

From a doctrinal standpoint, there are many biblical examples we could cite where we're told to "stand firm and hold fast" to the truths that Mary, the apostles, and all the saints hand on to us. But perhaps the best example of this is St. Paul's discussion of the celebration of the Eucharist and his emphasis on the doctrine of the Real Presence of Christ in the Eucharist:

> "Be *imitators* of me, as I am of Christ. I commend you because you remember me in everything and maintain the traditions even as I have delivered them to you. . . For I received from the Lord what I also delivered to you, that the Lord Jesus on the night when He was betrayed took bread, and when He had given thanks, He broke it, and said, 'This is my body which is for you. Do this in remembrance of me.' In the same way also the cup, after supper, saying, 'This cup is the new covenant in my blood. Do this, as often as you drink it, in remembrance of me.' For as often as you eat this bread and drink the cup, you proclaim the Lord's death until He comes" (1 Cor. 11:1, 23-26).

Other biblical passages that undergird the Catholic practice of meditating on the lives of Mary and the saints and striving to imitate them are Galatians 1:24, 4:12 and Hebrews 11:1-140, 12:1-2.

An Historical Example

As the Catholic faith spread across North Africa and

the Mediterranean world in the first five centuries after Christ's Resurrection, the Catholic Church was constantly under attack — physically or theologically — from one group or another. In the face of theological challenges from sects and competing religions, Catholic doctrines were constantly in need of clear and vigorous exposition by theologians and apologists.

Most of the early heresies were Trinitarian and Christological in nature, but there was, early on, a now obscure heresy that sought to deify the Blessed Virgin Mary. This movement was known as Collyridianism.

Little is known about Collyridian theology — few of the early Church Fathers mention the sect, even indirectly — and what little we do know is sketchy and very general. Not even the names of the group's leaders are mentioned by writers of the time. But one thing we *do* know for sure from the evidence that does exist: The early Church was horrified by the very idea of a Christian worshipping Mary or in any way rendering to her the adoration (Greek: *latria*) due to God alone. Such horror should be the reaction of any Catholic today when faced with a similar problem. An examination of the Collyridian heresy will serve as a reminder for us today the Catholic Church's strenuous teaching that we should honor and venerate Mary, but never adore her (or any other creature).[115]

The Collyridians were known for their excessive Marian devotion which developed into the outright

---

[115] Cf. CCC 971, 2110-2114.

idolatry of "Mary worship." This aberration grew out of the Church's rightful veneration of Mary as ever-virgin, Mother of God, and powerful heavenly inter-cessor, but it crossed the line of orthodoxy when certain Christians began to worship Mary as divine. Although details about the Collyridians are scanty, one of the few specifics we know of them is that at their liturgical service, bread was offered as a sacrifice to Mary. The historical evidence shows a strong and widespread practice of orthodox devo-tion to Mary (described by the theologians of that day as *hyperdulia*: a Greek term meaning the highest form of veneration that can be offered to a creature) by the 300s, but it's remarkable that very few dis-putes arose on issues pertaining directly to her or her role in the Church.

One that did spring up was a fourth-century at-tack by a writer named Helvidius, who wrote against the universal Catholic belief in Mary's per-petual virginity. (But this novelty was vigorously re-futed by Jerome and other key theologians). In fact, the officially defined Marian doctrines that were promulgated by early Church councils, eg. Mary's status as *Theotokos* (Greek for God-bearer), arose out of the Church's desire to settle Christological disputes, not in an effort to deal directly with Marian issues.

The Collyridian heresy was simple: It promoted the worship of Mary. This was in direct conflict with the Catholic Church's condemnation of idolatry, as well as the Lord's condemnation (Ex. 20:3-5). This proscription applied not just to statue worship, but to the worship of anything besides God.

The Catholic Response

It's ironic that the most diligent opponent of the Collyridians was St. Epiphanius (315-403), the bishop of Salamis. He was widely renowned for his learning and holy asceticism and was a close friend of St. Jerome, but he was also a rude and querulous man who garnered many enemies, a large number of whom were fellow Catholic bishops.

Though Epiphanius' efforts to squash the Collyridians were laudable, and his theological and scriptural reasoning against their idolatry was sound, he himself was not free from all error in the area of honoring God's friends. The vehemence of his opposition to the Collyridians' idolatry was rivaled by his fanatical opposition to icons. Patristics scholar Aloys Dirksen, C.P.P., provides a vivid description of Epiphanius, reminiscent of certain modern-day Evangelical foes of Catholic Marian doctrines:

> "[Epiphanius had a] fiery temperament and unreasonable impetuosity . . . that made the calm objectivity necessary for scholarly work impossible for him. His narrow-mindedness is apparent in the part he played in the Origenist controversy and the violence with which he attacked the veneration of images. He considered this idolatry, and in his testament he anathematized anyone who would even gaze upon a picture of the Logos-God.
> . .
>
> "His temperament made him suspicious of heresy

everywhere, and he made capital of even the smallest inaccuracy of statement. It appeared impossible for him to see any viewpoint but his own. Since he lacked critical acumen and was a poor, even a tiresome writer, his works would be of little value if it were not for his many quotations. He thus saved much that would otherwise have been lost to us."[116]

Epiphanius wrote against the Collyridians in his apologetics work, *Panarion* (Greek: *Medicine Box* [A.D. 374-377]), a tour-de-force refutation of more than eighty heresies he was aware of. Interestingly, he refuted the two extreme and diametrically opposed Marian heresies of his day, Collyridianism (which overly exalted Mary) and Antidicomarianitism, an Arabian movement that debased Mary's status and virtues, to the point of claiming "that holy Mary had intercourse with a man, that is to say, Joseph, after the birth of Christ."[117]

The Collyridians were mainly women, who developed a syncretistic combination of Catholicism and pagan Goddess cult customs. After describing the "awful and blasphemous ceremony" in which these women would adorn a chair or a square throne and spread a linen cloth over it for their ritual, Epiphanius writes,

> "Certain women there in Arabia have introduced this absurd teaching from Thracia: how they offer up a sacrifice of bread rolls in the name of the

---

[116] Aloys Dirksen, *Elementary Patrology* (St. Louis: Herder, 1959), 117.
[117] *Panarion* 78:1.

Ever-Virgin Mary, and all partake of this bread."[118]

He emphasizes the difference between Mary (the holiest, most perfect creature, but a creature nonetheless), and God:

> "It is not right to honor the saints beyond their due . . . Now the body of Mary was indeed holy, but it was not God; the Virgin was indeed a virgin and revered, but she was not given to us [by God] for worship, but she herself worshipped Him who was born in the flesh from her. . . Honor Mary, but let the Father, the Son, and the Holy Spirit be worshipped, but let no one worship Mary . . even though Mary is most beautiful and holy and venerable, yet she is not to be worshipped."[119]

The bottom line is this: Anyone who worships Mary or any other creature is committing idolatry and must be rebuked. We should look to Scripture, at the case of the angel who rebuked John for his temptation to idolatry, to see how to admonish modern-day Collyridians:

> "At this I fell at his feet to worship him. But he said to me, 'Do not do it! I am a fellow servant with you and with your brothers who hold to the testimony of Jesus. Worship God!'" (Rev. 19:10).

Our Lady herself would say this to any who would seek to worship her.

---

[118] Ibid. 78:13.
[119] Ibid. 78:23; 79:1, 4.

Appendix

The Council of Trent: "Decree Concerning the Invocation, Veneration, and Relics of Saints, and on Sacred Images"

(Issued at Session 25, December 4, 1563.)

THE HOLY COUNCIL commands all bishops and others who hold the office of teaching and have charge of the *cura animarum* (care of souls), that in accordance with the usage of the Catholic and Apostolic Church, received from the primitive times of the Christian religion, and with the unanimous teaching of the holy Fathers and the decrees of sacred councils, they above all instruct the faithful diligently in matters relating to intercession and invocation of the saints, the veneration of relics, and the legitimate use of images, teaching them that the saints who reign together with Christ offer up their prayers to God for men, that it is good and beneficial suppliantly to invoke them and to have recourse to their prayers, assistance and support in order to obtain favors from God through His Son, Jesus Christ our Lord, who alone is our redeemer and savior; and that they think impiously who deny that the saints who enjoy eternal happiness in heaven are to be invoked, or who assert that they do not pray for men, or that our invocation of them to pray for each of us individually is idolatry, or that it is opposed to the word of God and inconsistent with the honor of the one mediator of God and men, Jesus Christ,[120] or that it is foolish to pray vocally or mentally to those who reign in heaven.

Also, that the holy bodies of the holy martyrs and of others living with Christ, which, were the living members of Christ and the temple of the Holy Ghost,[121] to be awakened by Him to eternal life and to be glorified, are to be venerated by the faithful,[122] through which many benefits are bestowed by God on men, so that those who maintain that veneration and honor are not due to the relics of the saints, or that these and other memorials are honored by the faithful without profit, and that the places dedicated to the memory of the saints for the purpose of obtaining their aid are visited in vain, are to be utterly condemned, as the Church has already long since condemned and now again condemns them.

Moreover, that the images of Christ, of the Virgin Mother of God, and of the other saints are to be placed and retained especially in the churches, and that due honor and veneration is to be given them; not, however, that any divinity or virtue is believed to be in them by reason of which they are to be venerated, or that something is to be asked of them, or that trust is to be placed in images, as was done of old by the Gentiles who placed their hope in idols;[123] but because the honor which is shown them referred to the prototypes which they represent, so that by means of the images which we kiss and before

---

[120] Cf. 1 Tim. 2:5.
[121] Cf. 1 Cor. 3:16, 6:19; 2 Cor. 6:16.
[122] Cf. 2nd Council of Nicea, canon 7.
[123] Cf. Ps. 134:15 ff.

which we uncover the head and prostrate ourselves, we adore Christ and venerate the saints whose likeness they bear. That is what was defined by the decrees of the councils, especially of the Second Council of Nicea, against the opponents of images.

Moreover, let the bishops diligently teach that by means of the stories of the mysteries of our redemption portrayed in paintings and other representations the people are instructed and confirmed in the articles of faith, which ought to be borne in mind and constantly reflected upon; also that great profit is derived from all holy images, not only because the people are thereby reminded of the benefits and gifts bestowed on them by Christ, but also because through the saints the miracles of God and salutary examples are set before the eyes of the faithful, so that they may give God thanks for those things, may fashion their own life and conduct in imitation of the saints and be moved to adore and love God and cultivate piety.

But if anyone should teach or maintain anything contrary to these decrees, let him be anathema. If any abuses shall have found their way into these holy and salutary observances, the holy council desires earnestly that they be completely removed, so that no representation of false doctrines and such as might be the occasion of grave error to the uneducated be exhibited.

And if at times it happens, when this is beneficial to the illiterate, that the stories and narratives of the Holy Scriptures are portrayed and exhibited, the people should be instructed that not for that reason is the divinity represented in picture as if it can be seen with bodily eyes or expressed in colors or figures. Furthermore, in the invocation of the saints, the veneration of relics, and the sacred use of images, all superstition shall be removed, all filthy quest for gain eliminated, and all lasciviousness avoided, so that images shall not be painted and adorned with a seductive charm, or the celebration of saints and the visitation of relics be perverted by the people into boisterous festivities and drunkenness, as if the festivals in honor of the saints are to be celebrated with revelry and with no sense of decency.

Finally, such zeal and care should be exhibited by the bishops with regard to these things that nothing may appear that is disorderly or unbecoming and confusedly arranged, nothing that is profane, nothing disrespectful, since holiness becometh the house of God.[124]

That these things may be the more faithfully observed, the holy council decrees that no one is permitted to erect or cause to be erected in any place or church, howsoever exempt, any unusual image unless it has been approved by the bishop; also that no new miracles be accepted and no relics recognized unless they have been investigated and approved by the same bishop, who, as soon as he has obtained any knowledge of such matters, shall, after consulting theologians and other pious men, act thereon as he shall judge consonant with truth and piety.

But if any doubtful or grave abuse is to be eradicated, or if indeed any graver question concerning these matters should arise, the bishop, before he settles the controversy, shall await the decision of the metropolitan and of the bishops of the province in a provincial synod; so, however, that nothing new or anything that has not hitherto been in use in the Church, shall be decided upon without having first consulted the most holy Roman pontiff.[125]

---

[124] Cf. Ps. 92:5.
[125] H.J. Schroeder, O.P., editor and translator, *Canons and Decrees of the Council of Trent* (Rockford: TAN Books and Publishers, 1978), 215-217.

About the Author:

PATRICK MADRID is the publisher of *Envoy* magazine, an award-winning Catholic journal of apologetics and evangelization. He is the author of *Surprised by Truth* and *Pope Fiction*, along with the Surprised by Truth series, *Where Is That In the Bible?*, *Search and Rescue*, and *Why Is That In Tradition?* He is also the host of two EWTN television series: "Pope Fiction" and "The Truth About Scripture and Tradition." Patrick and his wife Nancy have been blessed with eleven children. Information about his work in apologetics is available at www.surprisedbytruth.com.

Envoy Magazine
P.O. Box 1117
Steubenville, OH 43952
800-55-ENVOY
www.envoymagazine.com
patrick@surprisedbytruth.com

How to Order

CATHOLIC WORD
Bringing You The Best in Catholic Publishing

Ascension Press, Basilica Press, Lilyfield Press,
St. John Press & Company Publications

W5180 Jefferson St.   Phone: 800-933-9398
Necedah, WI 54646   Fax: 608-565-2025
                        Email: familytrad@aol.com

PO#:_____   Date:_____

Bill To: **Ship To:**

Name:_____   Name: _____
Address:_____   Address: _____
City:_____ State:___ Zip:_____   City:_____State:___ Zip:_____
Phone:_____ Fax:_____
Email: _____

QTY	ISBN	Case	Description	Unit Price	Total
	096-592-2812	20/81	Friendly Defenders Catholic Flash Cards $11.99 NEW!		
	096-592-2804	36	Did Adam & Eve Have Belly Buttons? $12.99		
	096-592-2820	32	The Rapture Trap $11.99 NEW!		
	096-426-1081	40	Surprised By Truth $14.99		
	097-035-8903	44	My Life on the Rock $14.99		
	096-426-1006	28	Pope Fiction $14.99		
	096-426-1065	44	Making Senses Out of Scripture $14.95		
	096-426-1022	72	Nuts and Bolts $11.95		
	193-031-4078	34	Scripture Studies - Galatians $14.95		
	193-031-4000	16	Bible Basics $19.95		
	096-426-109X	84	Any Friend of God's Is A Friend of Mine $9.95		
	096-426-1030	60	Springtime of Evangelization $14.95		
	193-031-4019	36	Lessons from Lives of the Saints $12.95		
	096-714-9215	48	Philadelphia Catholic in King James's Court $12.95		
	096-714-9223	120	Philadelphia Catholic Discussion/Study Guide $3.95		
	093-898-4047	30	Holy Innocents: A Catholic Novel $16.95 NEW!		
	096-701-0209	60	Triumph of God's Kingdom in the Millennium and End Times $14.95		
				Subtotal	
				Shipping	
				Total	

Notes: _____
_____
_____

Call for Bookstore & Parish Discounts

Include $4 for the 1st book and $.50 for each additional book or call for
exact shipping.

Do you know someone whose Catholic Faith ended here?

If you're like most Catholics, your answer is "yes", a family member, friend, or co-worker.

Now you can do something about it. You can bring them home to the Church with *Envoy* magazine, an exciting bi-monthly journal of Catholic apologetics and evangelization.

Published by Patrick Madrid, best-selling Catholic author of books like *Surprised by Truth, Surprised by Truth 2, Pope Fiction and Where Is that In the Bible? Envoy* magazine will teach you how to explain and defend Catholic truth in a way that works. Each issue gives you cutting-edge information and answers from today's top Catholic apologists, evangelists, and writers. Our articles are consistently fresh, upbeat, useful, and *charitable*.

Envoy magazine will show you how to explain your Catholic Faith intelligently, defend it charitably, and share it *effectively*. It will prepare you to be an ambassador for Christ.

Subscribe today, and the next time you're faced with friends or loved ones who have lost their Catholic Faith (if not their First Communion picture), you can answer their questions and be a light to guide them home.

Bringing Christ to the World

Call 1-800-55-ENVOY - www.envoymagazine.com

Parish and RCIA bulk quantities available.